ELEANOR ROOSEVELT'S NIGHTLY PRAYER

ELEANOR ROOSEVELT'S NIGHTLY PRAYER

THE RELIGIOUS LIFE *of the* FIRST LADY *of the* WORLD

DONN MITCHELL

The prayer often attributed to Eleanor Roosevelt (p. 2) was written by the Reverend Oliver J. Hart, rector of St. John's, Lafayette Square, from 1934 to 1940, and delivered during inaugural prayer services for Franklin Delano Roosevelt. Eleanor Roosevelt so loved the prayer that she shared it with the country by way of her syndicated "My Day" newspaper column.

Morehouse Publishing
19 East 34th Street
New York, NY 10016
www.churchpublishing.org

Morehouse Publishing is an imprint of Church Publishing Incorporated.

Cover design by David Baldeosingh Rotstein
Typeset by Westchester Publishing Services

Library of Congress Control Number: 2025941032

For my lifelong friend Catherine Harper Richardson, and my godson, Gavin James Riggall, both of whom helped to make this book possible.

CONTENTS

INTRODUCTION

On many occasions when I told people I was planning to write a book about the religious life of Eleanor Roosevelt, invariably I received one of two reactions. The first was "I didn't think she *was* religious." The second was "Don't you want to say 'spiritual' rather than 'religious'?"

The short answers are yes and no. Yes, she *was* religious, and no, "spiritual" fails to see the communal dimension of her life as a Christian.

On the dedication page of his book *Mother R*, Elliott Roosevelt described his mother as a "woman of faith."[1] Eleanor Roosevelt was baptized and buried in the Episcopal Church and made no secret of her lifelong adherence to it. Yet many people would not describe her as "religious," largely because her biographers mostly do not examine her participation in a community of faith and because she does not conform to any of the stereotypes associated with that term.

The failure to explore her religious heritage and its significance to her life and work is not unique to Eleanor Roosevelt scholars. Political historians generally tend to marginalize religion, suggesting, often with no evidence, that it had little or nothing to do with the life trajectory of their subject. They deem it unimportant or ignore it altogether if their person of interest does not embody any of the popular stereotypes about "religious" people: 1) the narrow-minded, judgmental *busybody*; 2) the sheltered, easily shocked *naïf*; 3) the otherworldly *spook*; or 4) the *fanatic*—irrational, driven, and uncompromising.

Eleanor Roosevelt, of course, was none of these things. If she had been, she could never have gained the trust and respect of those whom she influenced and those whom she helped. And they were legion. Over the course of her life, she wrote twenty-seven books and eight thousand newspaper and magazine columns, in addition to delivering more than one thousand speeches. While she was doing all of this, she served on committees and boards and organized countless activities intended to build friendships among people who needed to understand each other. Arguably, the most significant of these activities was her work as chair of the committee that produced the Universal Declaration of Human Rights, the world's most comprehensive and widely agreed statement of how we human beings should treat one another.

Because none of these activities was organized or sponsored by a religious group, it is easy to lose sight of Eleanor

Roosevelt as a Christian woman working through community organizations.

Another problem in political historiography is the tendency to understand religion solely as *belief*, a subjective embrace of an ideology or dogma. Absent is the communal dimension and any interpretation of the relevance of communal *praxis*, i.e., the everyday aspects of participation in a faith community: the worship life, the service projects, the educational activities, the casual conversations over coffee, the bake sales, the shared dinners, the shared taxicabs—all of which are part and parcel of the amorphous category of "religion."

Even Harold Ivan Smith's excellent book, *Eleanor: A Spiritual Biography*, the only book to take an in-depth look at any aspect of her religious life, views it through a psychological lens almost to the exclusion of the communal dimension.

The contemporary preference for discussing spirituality rather than religion, noted earlier, stems from both long-standing American individualism and from an anti-organization bias in contemporary culture. These tendencies impoverish our ability to understand the interplay of religion and public affairs. We want to find an individual with intense personal convictions rather than an individual supported by a community of shared values.

All human beings have spirituality. They do not all have religion. The ability to experience love and emotion, to perceive beauty, to imagine other realities, and to be moved by symbol are capabilities all people have, but they are inherently *subjective*, so much so that adequate language sometimes cannot be found to describe them to each other.

A parallel exists in the world of language and communication. All human beings have the ability to make sounds. Not all have language. When a baby cries, it requires an astute parent or caregiver to interpret the meaning of the utterances. Language is a means of organizing sounds and symbols into a comprehensive system of *objective* meaning. Once the baby has acquired language, it can communicate a subjective thought—"I'm hungry"—by objective means so that others around it can understand what the subjective thought is.

Like language, religion organizes subjective spiritual experiences into an objective symbol system that may be unintelligible to many but can be learned by all, in the same way that a language other than your own will be unintelligible unless you learn to speak and write it.

In the preface to her autobiography, Eleanor herself suggested the desirability of a less subjective or individualistic approach to a person's life story: "A real picture of any human being is interesting in itself, and it is especially interesting when we can follow the play of other personalities upon that human being and perhaps get a picture of a group of people and of the influence on them of the period in which they lived."[2] Perhaps she would agree that an exploration of a person of faith should include an exploration of the community that embraces that faith.

An additional problem with the tendency to reduce religion to dogma is that it misses the narrative dimension of religion. Christianity, like most of the world's religions, is a collection of stories that feed into a larger story in the same way that many streams, some quite beautiful in their own right, flow into a mighty river. Even the historic creeds of the Christian church are mostly narratives, very short summaries of "what happened." Doctrines, such as the Virgin Birth or the Second Coming, can be inferred from them, but the overall pattern is a tightly summarized story. Narrative theology suggests that *stories*, rather than *propositions*, are the most effective ways to communicate religious truth. They may also be the most effective way to understand religious people.

George Stroup and James W. McClendon Jr. are two theologians who believe narrative theology has specific implications for biography. It is important, they suggest, to "know what happens when an individual life story intersects or 'collides' with the communal story. In what sense are people's lives governed by root metaphors supplied by Christian tradition?"[3]

Such an approach could be an invaluable aid to our understanding of one of the most noteworthy lives of the twentieth century, but most of the scholarship on Eleanor Roosevelt gets nowhere near that concept. Yet, early in life she had a kind of death and resurrection experience, which could be interpreted as an intersection with the larger Christian story.

The loss of a parent is one of the worst fears a young child has. Eleanor lost *both* her parents by the time she was ten years old. Her mother died when she was eight. About two years later, a younger brother died, and then before the year was out, her father had died too. This painful stretch of time could be compared to Christ's agony on the cross. The next five years of her life, based on the way she describes them, would be analogous to a long time in the tomb. Then at the age of fifteen, when she is sent abroad for school, she has a kind of resurrection experience becoming once again the fascinating person her father believed she was. Eleanor believed in resurrection, and her life story is a story of a resurrected life.

Another obstacle to appreciation of Eleanor's religious life is America's pervasive cynicism about "politicians." Traces of it can be found in writings and political rhetoric from the Gilded Age when Eleanor was born, as people attempted to explain, if only to themselves, the rampant corruption of the era. But there was another view embraced by the Progressive Movement and other reform efforts that sought to expose, challenge, and eradicate corruption. The development of the civil service system, with its high view of public service, was one of the successes of these efforts.

Today, however, even the civil service itself is excoriated along with the "politicians" thought to indulge it. Threats to abolish, punish, or otherwise constrain the "deep state" are common. The idea that people with noble aspirations work selflessly for the common good is "laughed to scorn," as the psalmist would say. Nobody sincerely believes anything, it is said. Everything is "calculus." The agenda is to get power or to stay in power. Exhibiting any kind of religious sensibility or commitment to a particular tradition is probably just another attempt to curry favor or win votes, in this view.

Eleanor Roosevelt was *not* a politician. She never sought nor served in electoral office. But as the wife of one of the twentieth century's consummate political leaders, she is seen as a political figure, and, of course, she was eventually appointed to a diplomatic post by her husband's successor, President Harry Truman. Yet one clergyman who knew her personally expressed a different view. The Reverend J. H. Randolph Ray, one-time rector of New York's Little Church Around the Corner, said Mrs. Roosevelt seemed to be "almost completely without ambition or self-seeking," two qualities usually associated with politicians. Writing in the 1950s when Eleanor was actively promoting the cause of the United Nations, Ray suggested that only history would be able to estimate her value.[4]

Can the passage of time, coupled with an understanding of how Eleanor Roosevelt's life story intersected with the story of the Christian community, help us to see her more fully? Can we detect the "root metaphors" of Christianity and, specifically, Anglicanism in her life's work?

If the answer is to be yes, it will require us to reject a common assertion that she "overcame" a narrow religious upbringing to become a great humanitarian. It will also require us to reject the notions that she was only a nominal or "cultural" Episcopalian, connected to the church perhaps for reasons of social propriety, but not very serious or credulous about what the church taught. Both interpretations are put forward by a variety of biographers.

And both, as we shall see, are patently wrong.

CHAPTER ONE

A WOMAN OF FAITH

ELEANOR ROOSEVELT'S SON, ELLIOTT, recalled his mother's nightly routine. Seated at the typewriter in her bedroom, clad in her old blue robe, she would crank out another issue of her daily syndicated newspaper column, "My Day." Read by millions of Americans and carried by ninety newspapers at its height, she began the column in December 1935 at the age of fifty and continued writing it six days a week for the rest of her life, cutting back to three days only in her last two years. In many ways it was a prototype of today's "blogs," a publicly accessible diary with philosophical observations thrown in. Over the years, Mrs. Roosevelt routinely mentioned Jesus Christ in her columns and other writings and spoke to the intersection of faith and public life.[1]

At other times, the column might have to wait until morning while she spent the last hour of her day signing and often adding handwritten notes to letters typed earlier in the day. Upon completion of her day's work, according to Elliott, his mother would walk across the room and kneel beside her bed to offer the following prayer:

> Our Father, who has set a restlessness in our hearts and made us all seekers after that which we can never fully find, forbid us to be satisfied with what we make of life. Draw us from base content and set our eyes on far-off goals. Keep us at tasks too hard for us that we may be driven to thee for strength. Deliver us from fretfulness and self-pitying; make us sure of the good we cannot see and of the hidden good in the world. Open our eyes to simple beauty all around us and our hearts to the loveliness men hide from us because we do not try to understand them. Save us from ourselves and show us a vision of a world made new. May the spirit of peace and illumination so enlighten our minds that all life shall glow with new meaning and new purpose; through Jesus Christ our Lord. Amen.[2]

Although it had become part of her regular spiritual practice, the prayer was not her own composition. She explained in one of her columns that it had been part of a service in March 1940. "We all went at 10:30 to St. John's Church across Lafayette Square for the service which my husband always liked to have on the anniversary of his first inauguration day. One prayer which was read made a deep impression on me." She passed it along in full, suggesting others might want to pray it as well.[3]

The prayer was written by the Reverend Oliver J. Hart, who was rector of St. John's from 1934 to 1940. Hart subsequently became bishop of Pennsylvania. It is not known how many of Eleanor's readers adopted the prayer for their own use, as she herself did, but clearly it could be prayed by any Christian and, with the omission of the phrase "through Christ our Lord," it could be prayed by non-Christians as well. It focuses on what we desire to be rather than on what we regret about our sins and failures.

The ability to distill a broad universal truth even when discussing specifically Christian concepts like Christmas or Easter was one of Eleanor Roosevelt's gifts and one that continues to mystify her biographers. Many of them assume she must have somehow "overcome" her allegedly narrow religious upbringing. The truth is that Eleanor Roosevelt's upbringing was anything but narrow, including its religious dimension. Many of her strongest convictions, such as her belief in democracy, were grounded in the teachings of Jesus, and it is possible to see the way in which family, clergy, and parish life encouraged that view.

The key to this mystery can be found in a detailed look at Eleanor Roosevelt's "formation" as a Christian. This approach will involve challenging the modern American tendency to prefer discussions of "spirituality" to discussions of "religion." Instead, it will focus on the nature of her religious community, the ways it provided civic leadership, and the ways in which it may have differed from other religious communities in her formative years.

Scholars of religion describe formation as a lifelong process that involves learning about faith, developing a relationship with God, and growing in spiritual maturity. It can include a variety of activities, such as prayer, study, and community participation. It can address specific aspects, such as *conscience formation*—how an individual's innate sense of right and wrong is refined and developed by family, teachers, role models, and the individual's own life experiences. *Faith formation*—how the individual comes to believe specific things—and *spiritual formation*—how the individual interprets, experiences, and communicates with the nonmaterial dimension of life—are also components of what might be included in the overall category of *religious formation*.

THE BELLE AND THE BON VIVANT

Anna Eleanor Roosevelt was born on October 11, 1884, to Anna Hall and Elliott Roosevelt, younger brother of Teddy, who would become president of the United States by the time Eleanor turned seventeen. The couple lived in midtown Manhattan, where they worshipped at Calvary Church, Park Avenue. Elliott had also built them a summer home at Hempstead, Long Island. Their summer parish would have been St. George's, Hempstead, where the Tory propagandist and first bishop of the Episcopal Church Samuel Seabury, had served as the third rector from 1742 to 1764.

Both of Eleanor's parents were serious Christians. Anna's mother had written to her on the eve of her wedding to Elliott, saying, "I pray you and Elliott to enter your new life with your hearts turned to God." Elliott wrote back, saying, "We both knelt before the Giver of every good and perfect gift and thanked Him, the source of perfect happiness, for His tender loving kindness to us." And both were intensely involved in the life of the city. Her mother was something of a belle of New York society.

"In that society you were kind to the poor, you did not neglect your philanthropic duties, you assisted the hospitals and did something for the needy," Eleanor said. "You accepted invitations to dine and to dance with the right people only, you lived where you would be in their midst. You thought seriously about your children's education, you read the books that everybody read, you were familiar with good literature. In short, you conformed to the conventional pattern."[4]

Eleanor's biographer and longtime friend Joseph Lash said Anna and her three sisters were all "society belles, and all were considered slightly but attractively mad. Anna was the most competent, and she was also a little cold. Elliott was all spontaneity and tenderness, while beneath her youth and beauty Anna was a creature of rules and form."[5]

Anna's father had insisted his daughters learn proper posture in the straight-backed style of the English aristocracy. Long walks in the country with a stick across their backs nestled in the crooks of their arms produced a graceful bearing that stood out among the young ladies of New York society. One society newspaper cited Anna as a good example of correct posture in an article that lamented the unfortunate stoop and slouch of other debutantes.[6]

The Roosevelt family was quite different from the Halls. Eleanor said her father's family was "not so much concerned with Society (spelled with a big S) as with people, and these people included newsboys from the streets of New York" and children with physical disabilities.[7]

The Roosevelts were among New York's earliest European settlers. They had been granted land during the period of Dutch rule in New Netherlands and were members of the Dutch Reformed Church, known today as the Reformed Church in America. However, with the advent of English rule in 1664, the Church of England displaced the Dutch Reformed Church as the established church. Coupled with frequent intermarriage between English and Dutch families, this change meant that many of the old "Knickerbocker" families found themselves with a foot in both denominations.

The Roosevelts were no exception. Elliott's father was Dutch Reformed, but his mother was an Episcopalian. Elliott joined the Episcopal Church, but his older brother Teddy stayed mostly in the Dutch Reformed fold. While a student at Harvard, Teddy had been such an enthusiastic church schoolteacher at Christ Church, Cambridge, that the rector encouraged him to become an Episcopalian. Teddy recused himself from teaching rather than take such a serious step! Edith, his second wife, however, was an Episcopalian. When they were in Oyster Bay, he worshipped with her and was ultimately buried from Christ Church, Oyster Bay.

Elliott Roosevelt was educated in part at St. Paul's School, one of several prestigious nineteenth-century Episcopal schools founded with a mission to raise up "leaders for the nation." (Groton, which FDR and his sons attended, was another.) While he had a reputation as something of a playboy, Elliott was nonetheless among the charter members of Trinity Church Association, which was formed in 1878 to expand the work of New York's Episcopal parishes among the poor. Although the Episcopal City Mission had been founded in 1831, the explosive growth of poverty in the late nineteenth century had overwhelmed the agency. More hands, more work, and more money were needed. Eleanor's father was one of the young men who stepped up to the plate. This group included his fifth cousin, James Roosevelt, the older half brother of Elliott's godson, Franklin Delano Roosevelt, who would be born a dozen years later. Working with other prominent laymen, the Trinity associates spurred the development of many parish "welfare" programs, fresh air homes, lodging houses, working men's clubs, and schools to meet special needs.[8]

All this effort had a salutary effect beyond the direct help it provided to New York's neediest citizens. Despite its long-standing reputation as the "church of the rich," by 1900 the Episcopal Church claimed a larger share of the city's poor than any other Protestant denomination. It was not just the generosity manifested in the substance of what was provided that accounted for this new allegiance among the poor. It was also the theological disposition of the church. Episcopalians did not subscribe to the idea that poverty was evidence of moral failure on the part of the poor. Consequently, their churches were the only ones within New York Protestantism that did not require a quid pro quo in exchange for assistance. Some groups wanted those they helped to "take the pledge" to abstain from alcohol. Others wanted a promise to bring the children to Sunday school and so on. With the exception of lodging, Episcopal Church programs were usually offered on a no-strings-attached, logical approach in a tradition that emphasized the God of grace rather than the God of judgment. It was about *helping* people, not *fixing* them.

At a very young age, Eleanor had already had significant exposure to this theological viewpoint and the activities that gave expression to it. She also had significant firsthand knowledge of the people these ministries helped. "Very early I became conscious of the fact that there were people around me who suffered in one way or another," she recalled. "I was five or six when my father took me to help serve Thanksgiving dinner in one of the newsboys' clubs which my grandfather, Theodore Roosevelt [Sr.] had started. He was also a trustee of the Children's Aid Society for many years."

Her father explained "that many of these ragged little boys had no homes and lived in little wooden shanties in empty lots, or slept in vestibules of houses or public buildings or any place where they could be moderately warm, yet they were independent and earned their own livings," she said.[9]

An aunt took her to the New York Orthopeadic Dispensary and Hospital, founded with the help of her Grandfather Roosevelt. She said her family continued to be deeply interested in its work.

She recalled seeing numerous little children in casts and splints. "I was particularly interested in them because I had a curvature myself and wore for some time a steel brace which was vastly uncomfortable and prevented my bending over."[10]

Her mother's brother and two sisters also took her to decorate Christmas trees in Hell's Kitchen, the neighborhood Leonard Bernstein would later immortalize in West Side Story, and to sing with other children at the Bowery Mission on the Lower East Side. Hell's Kitchen is located in Manhattan's West Thirties. The Halls and Roosevelts lived in Murray Hill in the East Thirties. The distance between the two neighborhoods can be walked in less than fifteen minutes, so young Eleanor was aware that poverty and need were very close at hand. She said these activities meant that even at an early age "I was not in ignorance that there were sharp contrasts, even though our lives were blessed with plenty."[11]

Among those blessings were trips to Europe, yet these experiences alone do not fully rebut the suggestion that she had had a narrow upbringing. Her life in the church tells us more.

THE VALORIZATION OF PUBLIC SERVICE

Soon after her birth, young Eleanor was baptized at Calvary Church, Park Avenue, by Henry Yates Satterlee. A prominent New York City rector, Satterlee would acquire national stature several years later when he was elected to become the first bishop of the newly created Diocese of Washington. The Episcopal Church's national governing body, the General Convention, had authorized the subdivision of the Diocese of Maryland to create a new diocese consisting of the District of Columbia and four counties in Maryland. The intent was to create a new diocese that could provide a platform for the church's witness in public life. It was hoped that the convention would also approve a provision whereby the bishop of Washington would automatically become the presiding bishop, re-titled as archbishop of the United States, in the same way that the archbishop of Canterbury automatically becomes primate of all England.

While this latter effort did not succeed, proponents were successful in obtaining authorization for the construction of the Cathedral Church of St. Peter and St. Paul to be a great house of prayer for the nation as a whole, something Pierre L'Enfant had envisioned in his original architectural design for the city. The choice of the name was telling. St. Peter, the first bishop of Rome, and St. Paul, Luther and Calvin's favorite biblical author, underscored the Episcopal Church's claim to be both Protestant and Catholic, and in the view of partisans of the day, the logical nominee to become the "Church of America." Relevant qualifications were thought to be its primitive Catholic heritage, its approach to scripture and reason, its breadth, its tolerance, and its practical genius. By the time Eleanor came of age, talk of competition among Christian denominations was seen as indelicate and, as the century progressed, impolitic as well. Eleanor spoke in the more generous language of ecumenism even before she became a public figure.

George William Douglas, who had studied both in Oxford and at the General Theological Seminary in New York, was an assistant at Calvary around the time that Eleanor was born. He would later go to become rector of St. John's, Lafayette Square, in Washington, and the most influential advocate for the creation of the cathedral.[12]

A congressional charter was obtained and, in 1907, when Eleanor was twenty-three years old, Satterlee would be joined by the president of the United States—Eleanor's Uncle Teddy—in laying the cornerstone of what came to be known as Washington Cathedral, often called the National Cathedral. Teddy Roosevelt and Henry Satterlee were well-acquainted by that time. Teddy had been police commissioner of New York City at the time of Satterlee's tenure at Calvary. He had stood as Eleanor's godfather when Satterlee baptized her.

There is no evidence that Eleanor's family or her rector had any notion that baby Eleanor was destined to become a national and world leader; nonetheless, she was ushered into the church by someone who understood the church's valorization of public leadership. While some might see it as mere coincidence, others might see it as a prophetic occurrence. Her next two rectors would both go on to become deans of New York's Cathedral of St. John the Divine, which like Washington Cathedral, was predicated on the idea that it was to be a "House of Prayer for All People" and a steward of civic life. Thus, her entire life in the church through young adulthood was guided by clergy who had a high view of service to the nation.

CALVARY CHURCH

Calvary Church was founded in 1832 on what was then Fourth Avenue in the Gramercy Park section of Manhattan's East Side, just south of Murray Hill where Eleanor lived for most of her childhood. The original building was replaced with a new one in 1848. Designed by James Renwick, the architect of St. Patrick's Cathedral and many other landmark buildings, the church featured two lacey pointed French Gothic spires atop two octagonal bases. Unfortunately, within twelve years, the spires had become unstable and had to be removed. The octagonal bases remained, and although the loss of the spires diminished the building's charm, it was still attractive enough to inspire the celebrated American Impressionist Childe Hassam to immortalize it as it appeared on a snowy day the year before Eleanor was born. Today, even the octagonal bases are gone, but the parish maintains a lively ministry in concert with St. George's, Stuyvesant Square, which had been J. P. Morgan's parish.

The novelist Edith Wharton, although baptized at Grace Church, is said to have spent her girlhood at Calvary.

Despite its blue-blooded pedigree, Satterlee's Calvary was abuzz with social mission when baby Eleanor arrived. Two missions serving the poor of Manhattan's East Side were created to supplement the work of an existing city mission sponsored by the parish. The Olive Tree Inn was created to offer temporary lodging to the poor. Other activities included a workingmen's club with three hundred members, and a ministry to women in prison. A coffeehouse, a free reading room, and a gymnasium and bowling alley rounded out the parish's work.

Calvary Church, Park Avenue, where Eleanor Roosevelt was baptized. The Church Missions House, to the left of Calvary, served as the first national headquarters of the Episcopal Church.
Credit: Photograph by Brown Brothers, 1906. Source: New York Public Library, Irma and Paul Milstein Division of United States History, Local History and Genealogy.

All of this service to the community stems from the Episcopal Church's teachings about *duty* to the community. A prolific writer, Satterlee published *Life Lessons of the Prayer Book* when Eleanor was just six years old. Undoubtedly, she would be expected to learn those lessons.

"As boys and girls begin to develop into manhood and womanhood," Satterlee explained in his introduction, "there are many lessons regarding the conduct of life which are of the highest importance, yet which are seldom or never imparted. . . . Life, with all its duties and responsibilities, will soon be thrust upon them, and too often it comes without any adequate preparation on their part to meet it." Satterlee said he was of the opinion that neither secular nor religious schools supplied what was needed. He said a course focusing on the Book of Common Prayer itself was the solution because the Prayer Book "follows the Christian life of the believer from the cradle to the grave."

He said the various offices (or services) of the Prayer Book "set forth the social as well as the religious obligations of the Christian life, and by studying closely these Offices we are brought, face to face, not only with the duties to GOD that our baptismal vows require, but also with the duties that, as parents and children, as brothers and sisters, as husbands and wives, as masters and servants, as citizens and Christians, we owe to one another; and the aim of this book is to bring out these life lessons from the Prayer Book in such a way that the rising generation may realize the great responsibility of life before the time of action arrives."[13]

Satterlee had been strongly influenced by the Oxford Movement, which was begun by theologians at Oxford University in England in the 1830s and sought to recover the Catholic heritage of Anglicanism. Featuring the writings of John Henry Newman, Edward Bouverie Pusey, John Keble, and others, it had become a worldwide movement by the time of Eleanor's birth. While controversial in many parts, it was especially well-received in the Diocese of New York, whose high church foundation relied on Catholic understandings of episcopacy and community as outward and visible signs of God's grace.

The movement encouraged a sacramental understanding of the church as a community gathered by Christ himself and through which God's grace is transmitted, rather than as an association of the like-minded. Consistent with this emphasis, the movement encouraged more frequent eucharistic worship, a pattern Eleanor maintained throughout her life. Of all the rites of the church, the Holy Communion most clearly portrays Christ as offering himself to the people who gather around the altar, a sacrificial offering for the whole community.

In many parts of the Anglican world before the Oxford Movement, Holy Communion was celebrated only once a month. By the end of the nineteenth century, though, it was common for parishes to offer at least one service of Holy Communion every Sunday, often in addition to a noncommunion service with a sermon. Satterlee's Calvary (and Eleanor's) was one of those parishes.

Henry Yates Satterlee, the rector of Calvary Church, baptized Eleanor in 1884. He went on to become the first bishop of Washington and laid the cornerstone of Washington Cathedral in 1907. Courtesy of Project Canterbury.

Young Eleanor's rector was also a strong advocate of women's professional ministry, which took the form in those days of ordaining or otherwise setting aside deaconesses, who did a wide variety of pastoral, social service, and educational work. Deaconesses were eventually recognized as part of the diaconate, but not until 1970. In her teenage years when she needed a chaperone to accompany her to Europe for school, Eleanor would hire a deaconess to travel with her.

With a liturgy that emphasized community as a gift from God, a Sunday school curriculum emphasizing duty to one's neighbor (i.e., social responsibility), and parents and close relatives who involved her in various forms of support for the less fortunate, it is not difficult to see how these elements combined to shape the conscience of a young girl who would grow up to make the well-being of the community, ultimately the whole world, a life priority. It is also not difficult to see how a godfather who served as police commissioner, then as state legislator, then as governor of New York, and finally as vice president and president of the United States would shape her view of the nobility of public service. Joseph Lash described Eleanor as a woman with a sense of "deep spiritual mission," comparing her to Saint Theresa.[14]

It is not necessary to imagine some "Aha!" moment when little Eleanor recognized a call to public service. A more productive enterprise is to consider the many ways she absorbed it from her environment. Snippets of sermons and lessons from Sunday school undoubtedly crept into discussions over Sunday dinner, supplementing things she had seen with her own young eyes. Surely the life of the parish and the emphases of the rector colored the broader milieu Anna and Elliott Roosevelt created for their children.

THE CHURCH OF THE INCARNATION

When Eleanor was eight years old, her mother died, and she was required to live with her Grandmother Hall. Two years later, her younger brother and her father died as well. After Eleanor began living with her grandmother, she began worshipping at the Hall family's in-town parish, the Church of the Incarnation on Madison Avenue, just three blocks from the Hall family home in Murray Hill. She would be confirmed there as a teenager.

Despite the tremendous disruption in her family life, the change of parishes may not have been all that significant. The messages, overt and subliminal, that young Eleanor received at Incarnation continued the emphasis on social responsibility and the call to Christian service she had heard at Calvary. Eleanor would continue her relationship with Incarnation through most of her adult life.

Located just one block from the mansion and celebrated library of J. P. Morgan, the Church of the Incarnation opened its present building in 1864. Designed by Emlen T. Littell, it was a neo-Gothic structure rich in visual appeal. Stained-glass windows by Edward Burne-Jones, Henry Holiday Company, and the William Morris Company, all of England, were complemented by works of the Americans John La Farge and Tiffany Glass and Decorating Company. Sculptures by Louis Saint-Gaudens (younger brother of Augustus) and David Chester French added to the abundant visual messages that could sometimes convey what preaching and teaching could not.

For twenty years before Eleanor's presence, the parish had been guided by Arthur Brooks, DD, brother of the celebrated Phillips Brooks, author of "O Little Town of Bethlehem," who would become bishop of Massachusetts.

The interior of the Church of the Incarnation in the early twentieth century where Eleanor Roosevelt was confirmed. Public Domain, 1909.

Arthur Brooks was a strong advocate of higher education for women. He said New York "offered to a woman everything but an education."[15] Brooks was instrumental in founding Barnard College, the sister institution to Columbia University, and served as its first chair. He also served on the hospital corporation for the Post-Graduate Hospital, now part of NYU Langone Medical Center. The hospital was one of Grandmother Hall's favorite philanthropies. She took Eleanor there to decorate the Christmas tree in the babies' ward.

Under his tutelage, the parish had developed a number of ministries. The Niobrara League, created the year before Eleanor was born, was a mission to American Indians. The next year, the parish created the St. Augustine League as a mission to African Americans. The Montgomery Memorial Society from 1874 was a mission to Mexicans. In 1882 the parish created the Bethlehem Day Nursery to care for the children of working women.

There was also the Ladies' Employment Society and the St. Luke's Society, supporting St. Luke's Hospital. For many years the parish offered Sunday afternoon services at the New York Skin and Cancer Hospital.

All of these ministries were running at full throttle when Eleanor began attending church there upon moving in with her grandmother. New activities continued to be developed when William Mercer Grosvenor succeeded Brooks upon the latter's death in 1895. Grosvenor would be Eleanor's rector for the next sixteen years, during which time she would spend three years in England for her education, have her formal debut to society, and marry Franklin Roosevelt.

The year after Eleanor began attending Incarnation, the parish inaugurated financial support for St. David's on 160th Street, another mission for African Americans. When Eleanor was nineteen, the parish opened a medical department providing a doctor and nurse to visit the homes of families in the parish's various missions. Eight years later, a parochial report would show a staggering two thousand office visits and house calls in a single year! The principal ailments were children's diseases, pneumonia, and tuberculosis. About the same time, the parish reported that some four hundred children had attended a summer school created for children who would otherwise have been on the street when school was out.

Grosvenor's activist orientation, so generously supported by his parishioners, was clear in a Thanksgiving Day sermon. "The Christian life can never be the life of a lotus-eater, who leaves all to fate and lets the world drift on, careless of its woes, listless concerning its wrongs and content to let all things remain as they are or fall into ruin and decay. There is always an aggressive, eager activity about this new faith in Christ. It is a new life; it is like a fresh, powerful energy springing into a powerful life. It was a revelation that turned the world upside down by the new spirit that it put into all truth. Always, everywhere, it was life abounding more and more."[16]

The record does not establish whether Eleanor was present for that particular sermon, but it does help us see why her life in the church led her to see activism in community and public affairs as a necessary component of the Christian life. Another sermon provides further clues about what may have shaped Eleanor's thinking. "We know it is the duty of the Church of Christ to care for the poor, to defend the rights and liberties of the weak, to insist upon the just administration of law, and to denounce all fraud and all high-handed tyranny on the part of the rich and powerful."[17]

On another occasion, he suggested the "cold dogmatist, exact in creed, correct in logic, utterly orthodox in opinion, hurling the anathemas of the Church against all modern scholarship; or panic-stricken and faithless at every new thought that is born out of human knowledge, may utterly miss the presence of the Lord."[18] Eleanor's own tendency as an adult to forego the intricacies of doctrinal precision in favor of love and generosity was consistent with Grosvenor's view.

An echo of her rector's indifference to the "doctrinally correct" can be heard in this passage from Eleanor's 1940 book, *The Moral Basis of Democracy*: "Each man may have his own religion; the church is merely the outward and visible symbol of the longing of the human soul for something to which he can aspire and which he desires beyond his own strength to achieve."[19]

She went on to assert that a "Christ-like" way of life was essential for democracy. She defined this Christ-like way as one that cultivated a sense of obligation to live with a deeper interest in the welfare of one's neighbor. She said it was not necessary to actually *be* a Christian, but that it *was* necessary to acknowledge that the life of Christ was based on principles *necessary* for democracy.

"The citizens of a democracy must model themselves on the best and most unselfish life we have known in history. They may not all believe in Christ's divinity, though many will, but his life is important simply because it becomes a shining beacon of what success means."[20]

In other words, society does not have to be *Christian*, but it does have to be *Christ-like*. As a cradle Episcopalian, she may not have realized how characteristically Anglican this view was. It was an understanding that had been articulated for her from her earliest memory.

On another occasion Grosvenor told the church the birth of Christ must mean "for us justice to the oppressed, pity for the poor, compassion for those that are ignorant and out of the way; that strict honesty that protects the rights of others, that pushes the greed of gain aside, that with honest toil and honest reward the people may have the chance to live."[21]

It's not possible to say how all this mission activity and preaching about social responsibility might affect a ten-year-old girl dutifully sitting in her pew, but anyone familiar with the text of the Universal Declaration of Human Rights can see the ways in which it incorporates concepts Eleanor was taught at a very young age.

THE AESTHETIC DIMENSION OF RELIGION

Of course, teaching about and developing models of social responsibility was not the only thing the church had to offer. From her vantage point in the pew, Eleanor could see works of art depicting scenes that mattered to her personally. The stained-glass windows provide abundant examples.

One window by John La Farge commemorates the death of a child. When her little brother Elliott had died only two years after her mother's death, Eleanor wrote to her father saying she was confident they would both see Anna and little Ellie again. The La Farge window depicts young children as angels in the delicate, idealized style of Victorian romanticism, a comforting portrayal a child could appreciate.

Two William Morris Company windows also depict angels, these in the Pre-Raphaelite style associated with the Arts and Crafts Movement. They were given in memory of all infant children.

Still other windows reflected themes that would become important to Eleanor later in life. Above the altar three sets of clerestory windows by Henry Wynd Young depict Florence Nightingale wearing her nurse's cap and Saint Francis of Assisi holding a rabbit. Nursing would be an aspect of Eleanor's ministry in both world wars and during her husband's recovery from polio. As a peacemaker late in life, she took particular inspiration from the prayer attributed to Saint Francis and kept a copy close at hand.

As an adult, Eleanor's life would be the embodiment of faith and charity. In the nave two windows by Henry Holiday of London based on a design by Edward Burne-Jones show the Virgin Mary and Dorcas representing the two values. Dorcas, sometimes called Tabitha, was raised from the dead by Saint Peter and became known for her charitable works.

A Tiffany window depicted Jesus working in Joseph's carpenter shop in an affirmation of the dignity of labor, an affirmation Eleanor would take seriously when she joined the Women's Trade Union League and became an advocate for just and favorable labor conditions.

A Cottier and Company window combines the feeding of the five thousand and the provision of manna in the wilderness with the bread and wine of the Eucharist. Throughout her life, Eleanor was a provider of hospitality, an advocate of provision for the poor, and a reverent participant in the Eucharist.

With world-class art, celebrated preaching, energetic social service missions, and a family that supported all of it, why do historians persist in saying Eleanor had a "narrow" upbringing? The only plausible explanation is that they tend to zero in on the personality and eccentricities of a woman who had a very difficult responsibility thrust upon her late in life. Mary Hall, Eleanor's maternal grandmother, had already raised six children to adulthood when the oldest, Eleanor's mother, tragically died at the age of twenty-eight, leaving three children for Mrs. Hall to raise. Within two years, one of the children had also died—on her watch! A sympathetic eye can almost see the grip tightening as a well-intentioned, aging woman sought to protect her orphaned charges.

LIFE WITH GRANDMOTHER HALL

Eleanor lived with her grandmother from the time she turned eight until she went away to school at the age of fifteen. Mrs. Hall led a disciplined spiritual life and required her children and grandchildren to participate in daily Bible reading and formal household worship, as well as Sunday attendance at church. While formal, liturgical prayers are rare in American households today even among churchgoers, in the nineteenth century they were common among Christians. Returning to church on Sunday evening for a second worship service was also widespread. Those activities do not necessarily add up to "narrowness," even if they were required or the contemporary reader thinks them tedious.

Is it narrowness when a father encourages the family to gather around the television every Sunday to cheer a favorite team on to victory? If they followed suit every week, would we conclude that the family was narrowly focused on competitive sports? If we knew that some of the family members would rather be doing something else at that time, could we on that fact alone conclude that the father was a harsh disciplinarian?

The point here is that the charge of narrowness leveled by so many historians is more about the *proponent* of the activities than the activities themselves. In Eleanor's case, it's about Grandma.

While Mrs. Hall may have been a strict disciplinarian, that does not necessarily mean that she adhered to a "narrow" worldview or fundamentalist religion. Fundamentalism, as a religious movement, did not actually exist at the time she was caring for Eleanor. As her full name reveals, Mary Livingston Ludlow Hall was descended from the Livingston family, one of the Hudson River Valley's "first families." Her husband, Valentine Gill Hall Jr., had built their country home in Tivoli, New York, on a portion of the Livingston estate, which had been created through patents from Charles II, James II, and George I.[22]

Tivoli was hardly a backwater. Many of the Halls' neighbors and fellow parishioners at St. Paul's, Tivoli, such as the Clarksons and the DePeysters, were also descendants of "first families." All of them maintained town houses in New York City just as the Halls did, some of them in the same neighborhood of Murray Hill.

Despite the Hall family's comfort and social standing, it appears that the rigidity Eleanor recalled most likely originated with her grandfather, who died before she was born. While she did not know him personally, she did know he was an artist who did not have to work for a living and that his library contained many books on religion. With the exception of a hellfire-and-brimstone illustrated version of the Bible, which frightened her, Eleanor does not tell us anything more specific than that. Who were the authors of all the other books in the library? What were the topics? We are at the mercy of historians who conclude—possibly without having read any of them—that they must have been very narrow because Valentine Hall is said to have become very puritanical as time went by. It is suggested by some that he encouraged or possibly browbeat his wife into a similar frame of mind.

Mr. Hall was the grandson of Irish immigrants who may have had a Protestant background, which may well have included heavy doses of classical Calvinism with its harsh views of a "depraved" humanity requiring stern discipline. His father, Valentine Sr., however, was an active member of Calvary Church, which was already strongly involved in social mission in his day, and certainly did not center on Calvinistic thought. Therefore, it is probably fair to conclude that Valentine Jr.'s puritanism may indeed have been engendered or intensified by readings of his own choosing.

His wife most likely would not have chosen those readings and quite possibly did not explore them. Several authors note that Mary Hall's faith had different roots—a "God that appreciated joy and encouraged a wide appreciation of life and nature." This view is consistent with the general thrust of the Anglicanism in which she was raised. These same authors concluded that married life was not a pleasant experience for Eleanor's grandmother. Her husband lived off the family fortune and devoted his considerable time to religious study. While describing Mrs. Hall as deeply religious, these authors suggest that Valentine Jr. overruled his wife's faith and demanded that she and the family practice "the 'ramrod like self-denial' that he thought God demanded."[23]

One commentator described Mrs. Hall as a "fundamentalist Episcopalian."[24] This description is incorrect. Fundamentalism did not emerge as a movement until about the time of Mrs. Hall's death. And it never had a following in the Episcopal Church.

It might be more accurate to say she was a "literalist." Eleanor said her grandmother believed that every word in the Bible was literally true. (The adult Eleanor did not.)

This distinction is important because most Christians—Protestant, Catholic, or Orthodox—could have been described as literalists prior to the emergence in the late nineteenth century of the "higher criticism," which used archaeological discoveries and scientific concepts to challenge some biblical claims, such as the age of the earth and the occurrence of miracles. In some cases, it also provided verification of some events detailed in the sacred texts. The discovery of the Cyrus Cylinder, which we will discuss in chapter six, is an example.

Prior to the higher criticism, differences of opinion about scripture centered more on *authority* rather than literal truth. Luther and Calvin insisted that scripture was the sole and supreme authority on matters of the faith. Catholic and Orthodox theologians, on the other hand, maintained that the great tradition of the church had primary authority, because the Bible itself was a product of tradition. Anglicans argued that scripture and tradition were coequal with reason as sources of authority.

This distinction is consistent with distinctions in the Reformation itself. On the continent, the Reformation was about *theology*—right belief, right interpretation. The English Reformation was about *polity*. How should church and society be ordered? Should it be 1) a hierarchy of *persons* (favored by papists and advocates of episcopal polity); 2) a hierarchy of *councils* (favored by advocates of presbyterian polity); or 3) without hierarchy altogether (favored by congregationalists)? This concern traveled with Anglicanism through the centuries and across the oceans. In the time period when the higher criticism generated a reaction in the form of fundamentalism, Episcopalians were more likely to be caught up in debates about polity—high church, low church, broad church—and changes in ritual practice, innovations in the minds of some and restorations in the minds of others.

Fundamentalism developed mainly in Presbyterian circles and eventually led to multiple splits within Presbyterianism, eventually spreading to other denominations, but Eleanor's was not one of them.

When recalling her summers in Tivoli, Eleanor spoke of long, uncomfortable carriage rides to church on Sunday mornings. St. Paul's, though four miles from the Hall's country home, was also on the sprawling Livingston estate. Founded in 1816 by members of the Livingston family, St. Paul's was very much a part of the Diocese of New York, arguably the most racially, culturally, linguistically, and economically diverse US diocese at the time. Despite her years in Albany and Washington, Eleanor was a lifelong resident of the Diocese of New York.

While Eleanor may have chomped at the bit during her years in her grandmother's home, by the age of thirty-five, when she was well-established in her adult life, she was able to express a more considered view. Mary Hall died August 14, 1919. That night, Eleanor discussed her grandmother's death in her diary and called her "a gentle, good woman with a great and simple faith." Yet as much as she loved her grandmother, she had said on a number of occasions that as good a person as Mrs. Hall was, her life was neither happy, fulfilling, nor complete. "Her willingness to be subservient to her children isolated her," Eleanor said, "and it might have been far better, for her boys at least, had she insisted on bringing more discipline into their lives simply by having a life of her own." She said she had resolved, based on her grandmother's experience, to learn from the latter's sadness. "My grandmother's life had a considerable effect on me, for even when I was young," she wrote in *This I Remember*, "I determined that I would never be dependent upon my children by allowing all my interests to center in them."[25]

Eleanor would maintain her ties to her grandmother's parish, the Church of the Incarnation, throughout her life. In 1905 she would marry her fifth cousin once removed, Franklin Delano Roosevelt, adding the parish of his baptism, St. James' Church, Hyde Park, to her list of parish affiliations. Incarnation would be their in-town parish. A parochial report from 1912 records a generous contribution from the couple. When the president's mother died in 1941, her funeral would be at Incarnation. The parish built a ramp to accommodate FDR's wheelchair.

When Eleanor was twenty-seven, Franklin was elected to the New York State Senate. They took a house in Albany and began worshipping at Cathedral of All Saints, although they never cut their ties with either Incarnation or St. James', Hyde Park.

That same year, Grosvenor was called to serve as dean of the Cathedral of St. John the Divine, where one of his first sermons would ask, "Why is it we have so little respect for politicians? To serve the state is the noblest thing a man can do and yet we sneer at it and despise it."[26] It is hard to imagine that either Eleanor or Franklin Roosevelt would have disagreed.

Howard Chandler Robbins would succeed Grosvenor at Incarnation and later as dean of the cathedral. Hymnody and the early twentieth-century ecumenical movement were priorities for Robbins, who would play a leadership role in both hymnal revision and the Faith and Order Movement, an early precursor of ecumenical activity. He would cap his career as a professor at New York's General Theological Seminary.

The Roosevelts, however, were not present for much of Robbins's tenure. In 1913, President Woodrow Wilson appointed FDR as assistant secretary of the Navy. Eleanor's "Auntie Bye"—her father's sister, Anna—had a house in the Dupont Circle neighborhood of Washington, D.C. The couple borrowed the house and began worshipping at nearby St. Thomas' Church, where FDR would be elected to the vestry a few years later. Eleanor would enroll two of their sons at St. Alban's School on the close of Washington Cathedral, where Eleanor's baptismal priest, Henry Yates Satterlee, lay buried in the crypt of Bethlehem Chapel.

With a strong emphasis on women's ministry at Calvary and a strong emphasis on women's education at Incarnation and with both parishes valuing public service and committing to social mission, it is not difficult to see how Eleanor Roosevelt's religious formation gave rise to a distinguished life of public service, as she was always an advocate for the disadvantaged, for women, and for peace.

CHAPTER TWO

A RESTLESS HEART AND A SEEKER OF TRUTH

Eleanor Roosevelt's nightly prayer began "Our Father, who has set a restlessness in our hearts and made us all seekers after that which we can never fully find. . . ." One possible reason the prayer resonated with her so strongly when she first encountered it is that her own restless heart had been with her from birth. Her father had encouraged her sense of adventure but, alas, after his untimely death, it would be frustrated for many years before being unleashed again on the threshold of adulthood.

Another point of resonance would likely have been the notion that we are lifelong seekers. This concept fits well with the teachings of the Episcopal Church, which hold that salvation is a gradual, lifelong process rather than a once-and-done event. Growth and change are possible in this view. Not everything need be believed all at once—some things, perhaps, never. Other beliefs may be discarded at some point; still others discarded and later recovered on very different terms. Some beliefs may be doubted or poorly understood throughout life only to become profoundly meaningful at a later point. The relationship of this fluid, developmental understanding of belief to the larger heritage of Anglicanism will be considered in more depth later in the chapter.

ELLIOTT AND HIS LITTLE NELL

Eleanor adored her father. Elliott Roosevelt was debonair, handsome, and romantic. Regarded by many as a playboy, he nonetheless adored his "Little Nell," the nickname he chose for her and which she cherished. Part of what he gave her was a focused attention, which a friend of his sister, Corrine, described as an ability to shut out the rest of the world and make you feel as if you were the most important thing to him.[1] According to biographer Joseph Lash, Elliott presented Eleanor with the picture of "what he wanted her to be—noble, brave, studious, religious, loving, and good."[2]

She had fond memories of him from a family trip to Italy when she was six years old. "Some sort of fiesta was going on at the time and people were tossing flowers,"[3] she said, recalling their visit to Venice. Her father treated her to a gondola ride. "I remember my father acting as gondolier, taking me out on the Venice canals, singing with the other boatmen, to my intense joy. I loved his voice and, above all, I loved the way he treated me."[4]

Her memory suggests that he was able to work miracles for his little girl too. Three years earlier, she had been traumatized on an ocean voyage when the SS *Britannic*, carrying the Roosevelts, collided with the SS *Celtic*. All the passengers had to be evacuated. With her father standing in a lifeboat below, three-year-old Eleanor had to be dropped from an upper deck into her father's arms below.[5] Several biographers maintain that she had a lifelong fear of the water, but there she was three years later in a gondola being charmed by the dashing Elliott. She made many subsequent ocean voyages: for school, for her honeymoon, and for her UN work. She had a pool installed at her Val-Kill cottage and joined in swimming with family and friends who came over for picnics and summertime festivities, but there are reports that she resisted going on boat rides as a young girl.

Is this one of the many fears in her life she subsequently overcame? Or was it the safety of her father's gaze that made everything all right, providing a kind of permission to relish adventure? She remembered from that trip to Italy "standing on the edge of Vesuvius with him while he threw in a penny, which came back covered with lava. There was excitement and wonder in that. He took me through the ruins and showed me a petrified loaf of bread and told me how a long-vanished civilization had lived. But it wasn't dead history. It became vivid to me."[6] She said she came to see them as living people, as real to her as those around her.

Elliott Roosevelt with his "Little Nell," a favorite nickname for Eleanor. Courtesy of the FDR Library.

Elliott's adventuresome nature was evident well before Eleanor was born. When he was just twenty years old, he persuaded his older brother, Teddy, to join him on an expedition to India. In addition to rounds of big game hunting, the trip included abundant invitations to dinners and outings with India's princes and their British overlords. Despite admitting to his sister that he enjoyed their glamorous, polo-playing life, his social conscience had not been extinguished.

He lamented the "ocean of misery and degradation" he saw, suggesting that it might teach those who claim to care about humanity "to know new horrors and sadness that the mortal frames and still more the Immortal Souls of Beings in God's image made, should be brought so low. The number and existence of these some millions of poor wretches has upset many preconceived notions of mine."[7]

As much as he enjoyed fun and games, it seems, he never lost sight of everyday people. This was the lesson he taught Eleanor in the petrified ruins in Italy: no matter how remote in terms of history, social status, or geographical location, they are all "beings in God's image made."[8]

A HIDDEN AGENDA

Unfortunately, despite his compassion and moral insight, despite his charm and capacity for flamboyant adventure, there was a sadder tale. And on that very trip to Italy which Eleanor so fondly recalled, there was a hidden agenda beneath the merriment and exhilaration. For the wealthy, Joseph Lash points out, extended trips to Europe were often a subterfuge for finding a spa to "dry out" and avoid scandal back home.[9] Elliott needed help, and part of the reason for the trip was to find it.

Elliott's problems dated back to his teenaged years. After he finally succeeded in persuading his father to let him study at St. Paul's, he eventually had to withdraw from the school he so desperately wanted to attend. Although his academic work was well-regarded, he was plagued by headaches and seizures that ended in fainting. It was thought that he might have had a form of epilepsy, but specialists felt his condition did not conform to epilepsy's known symptoms. His condition, often accompanied by depression, never had a clear diagnosis. In the absence of effective treatment, he began at a young age an attempt to medicate the situation with alcohol, an easily disguised solution in his social circle.

The problem continued after he met Anna. He even had a seizure on one of his visits to Tivoli during their engagement. Still the couple was in love, and the families approved. The marriage proceeded, and Eleanor was the first of three healthy children born to the couple. But the year before the Italian holiday, Elliott's condition had worsened. He had broken his leg while rehearsing a stunt for an amateur circus. It is believed the physicians failed to set the leg properly, resulting in the need to break the leg again. The leg never healed completely, adding enduring pain to his still-recurring seizures. And Elliott added morphine and laudanum to his alcohol-driven "treatment plan."[10]

In desperate hope of finding a cure, Anna planned an Italian get-away. When the family left Italy, Anna rented a house in Neuilly, west of Paris, while Elliott entered a sanitarium in Vienna. At Neuilly, Anna gave birth to her third child, Eleanor's youngest brother, Hall. "Auntie Bye," Elliott's sister, came to stay with her. Young Eleanor was sent off to a convent, ostensibly to learn French, but in Eleanor's interpretation, to get her out of the way for a while.[11]

It was an unhappy experience.

"The little girls of my age in the convent could hardly be expected to take much interest in a child who did not speak their language and did not belong to their religion. They had a little shrine of their own and often worked hard beautifying it. I longed to be allowed to join them but was always kept on the outside and wandered by myself in the walled-in garden."[12]

Unhappy experience or not, it nonetheless challenges the notion that Eleanor's exposure to religion was narrow. Moreover, she did eventually become fluent in French as well as German.

Eleanor's relationship with her mother was significantly different from the joyous, playful relationship she had with her father. Anna had been quite frank in encouraging her daughter to see herself as "homely." It must have been a special annoyance to her that her daughter required a brace to correct a curvature when she herself was widely celebrated for her perfect posture and regal carriage. She sometimes called her daughter "Granny" because she thought her "too serious." Biographer Blanche Wiesen Cook suggests Anna may actually have been somewhat jealous of Elliott's affection for their daughter, since affection seems to be something that was lacking in their marital relationship.[13] Was it Anna's coldness or Elliott's drinking that caused the problem? Is it even possible to know? In the beginning of their relationship, however, Elliott seems to have been quite playful with Anna, and there appeared to be genuine affection between the two. But as his drinking and drug abuse progressed, there were also infidelities and even a child out of wedlock.[14]

Anna and the children returned to New York, but Elliott stayed behind, first for treatment, and then for an involvement with another woman. Although he eventually returned to New York, he never lived with the family again. Anna bought a house two blocks from Auntie Bye on the Upper East Side. Elliott visited the family when permitted, and he maintained a lively correspondence with Eleanor. There was talk of divorce, but it never came to pass. In the fall of 1892, Anna was stricken with diphtheria. She died in December of that year.

Although Elliott insisted he should have custody of his children, his Roosevelt siblings did not agree and supported the arrangements Anna had made before she died. The children were to be raised by their grandmother, Mary Hall.

Mrs. Hall allowed very few visits from Elliott, but the correspondence remained steady. It seems to be a major way that Eleanor coped with her grief. She wrote to her father about her confidence that they would see Anna again in heaven and she fantasized about she and her father someday living together and having adventures again. Elliott did not attempt to disabuse her of these ideas. But then tragedy struck again. In 1894, when Eleanor was ten, the older of her two brothers, Elliott Jr., also succumbed to a serious illness. Accounts vary as to whether it was diphtheria or scarlet fever, but Eleanor coped in the same way, expressing confidence to her father that they would be reunited with little Ellie as well. It seems it was her father who was unconsolable. His drinking intensified and in August of that year, in a vicious episode of delirium tremens, he jumped out a window. He survived the fall but died of heart failure on the night of August 14.

Eleanor said she kept the relationship alive through her imagination and the preservation of his letters. She is said to have carried them with her for the rest of her life.

A LONG PERIOD IN THE TOMB

Eleanor told Joseph Lash she had survived a "very miserable childhood." Her cousin Corinne Robinson Alsop concurred, saying, "It was the grimmest childhood I have ever known. Who did she have? Nobody."[15]

Grandmother Hall had a house on West Thirty-Seventh Street in Manhattan as well as the country estate at Tivoli. The town house was described as dark and unwelcoming, and Eleanor was rarely permitted to have friends in. Her education was mostly accomplished by tutoring for the next four years. She describes the pleasures of Tivoli more favorably, reveling in its natural beauty on the banks of the Hudson and happily finding trees she could hide behind when she wanted to read in seclusion.

Two of Anna's younger sisters and her two younger brothers still lived at home. Eleanor said her grandmother had been unable to provide discipline for her own children and so she doubled down on her grandchildren. Her two aunts were beautiful like their late sister and seemed

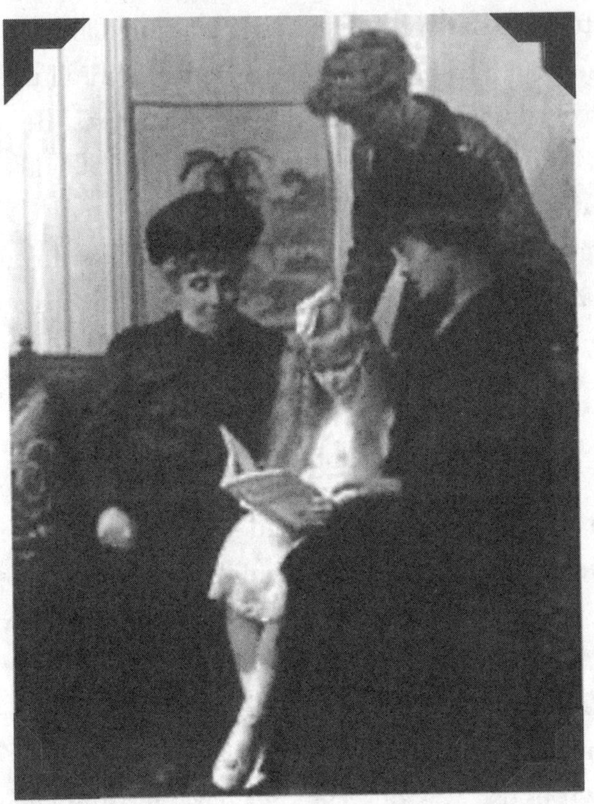

Grandmother Mary Hall, daughter Anna, ER, and Aunt Tissie, 1913. Courtesy of FDR Library.

destined to follow her glass-slippered footsteps into high society. Her two uncles were tennis bums, both with heavy drinking problems. When they were in the country, they sometimes amused themselves by pointing shotguns out their bedroom windows and firing at the feet of passersby. Eleanor had three locks on her bedroom door, ostensibly to keep the boys at bay.[16]

From age ten to fifteen, Eleanor's life consisted of highly structured routines in the home, a dearth of friendship and peer relationships, and a variety of tutors, some of whom she overtly detested. Historians generally agree that her most significant educational development occurred under the tutelage of Mademoiselle Marie Souvestre, headmistress of Allenswood Boarding Academy in Wimbledon, England, where Eleanor would begin studies at age fifteen. But there is at least one tutor who must also be credited for drawing out Eleanor's gifts as a writer. Between age seven and her departure for Allenswood, one of Eleanor's tutors had been Frederic Roser, a well-known tutor of the children of high society. Some of her cousins shared classes with her over the years, as well as Margaret Dix, daughter of Morgan Dix, one-time rector of Trinity Church, Wall Street.[17] None of them seemed to have anything especially nice to say about him. He appears to have lacked any warmth or congenial attributes.[18] He was very formal and strict in his academic approach. But the essays he required Eleanor to write demonstrate her gifts and her promise and his skill in drawing them out. He frequently remarked that a particular essay should be published. None were, but a few of them survive. One in particular seems to draw on multiple themes that were close to Eleanor's heart.

At the age of thirteen or fourteen, during the period Eleanor describes as miserable, "The Flowers Discussion" features Eleanor awaking from a nap in a conservatory where there were orchids, camellias, and other flowers growing. As she awoke she heard the flowers discussing who among them was the most beautiful. She pretended to still be asleep so she could hear the conversation. Different flowers made the case for why they were the most beautiful. For some it was color. For some it was graceful movement. For others it was fragrance. They try to use the choices made by visitors to the conservatory as proof, but in the end, the violet said that none of them was the most beautiful. "We are all beautiful in our own way. Some are beautifully colored. Others smell sweetly & again others are graceful. We were all made well. From this day we are all equal," the violet said. The other flowers then agreed from that day on they were equal. Eleanor concludes the essay on a personal note: "But I always have and always will love the violet best."[19]

It is not difficult to interpret Eleanor's thinking in this conclusion. After all of the emphasis on the beauty of her late mother and her aunts (and Eleanor's alleged deficiency in that regard), the violet's assertion that each flower is beautiful in its own way is more than just a nice resolution to an argument. Eleanor agrees with the violet. Even at this tender age, the blessedness of diversity and the equal worth of each one is an already deeply held value for her, one that may well have been critical to her psychological survival. But the question arises as to what may have been the inspiration for this essay. It may well have been an ingenious metaphor for a New Testament story Eleanor had heard often and was probably required to memorize. It appears in Matthew, Mark, and Luke and depicts the apostles arguing among themselves about who is the greatest among them.

Jesus tells them that the greatest must be the servant of all.[20] Everyone can be a servant. Everyone is great.

RESURRECTION

Eleanor's mother had expressed a wish on her deathbed heard by several family members. The wish was that Eleanor would be sent abroad to study. Mrs. Hall was not favorably disposed to the idea of Eleanor being so far from her watchful eye, but she felt her daughter's wishes took precedence over her own discomfort. Other members of the family agreed. Auntie Bye had studied under Marie Souvestre, a renowned French educator who had left her school in France and moved to England. The year before Eleanor was born, she had opened Allenswood Boarding Academy, an exclusive school for girls in Wimbledon. Other women in the Hall and Roosevelt social circles knew Mlle. Souvestre by reputation, and Eleanor's own parents had met her in France in 1891.[21] And so the die was cast. At the age of fifteen, Eleanor would travel to England to begin study under Mlle. Souvestre. All instruction would be in French, something that would not be a problem because Eleanor was fluent in French by this time. And her classmates would be girls of various nationalities from well-to-do, high-ranking families with well-known names such as Lloyd-George, Chamberlain, Strachey, and Webb.[22]

Eleanor's Aunt Tissie escorted her to England. For Eleanor, the experience of Allenswood was an experience of resurrection: "I can remember now the wonder and the freedom I experienced when I realized that I could start with a clean slate, that there was nothing to be afraid of."[23]

She said in the years since her father's death, she had not had "that sense of adequacy and of being cherished" until she met this teacher who would restore to her "some of the confidence which since my father's death I had not felt." Biographer Harold Ivan Smith said Eleanor thrived in this new environment. In both the classroom and among her peers, she was in every sense a success.[24]

In another context she said she felt she was starting a new life, "free from my former sins and traditions."[25] The only actual sin we know about comes from her admission in several places that she was in the habit of lying when she was too afraid to tell the truth. When she realized that all she had to do was obey the rules and tell the truth, the fear fell away, and, along with it, the dishonesty it generated. But she was freed of the things she imagined to be sins, at least in the sight of her mother and grandmother: her failure to be beautiful; her failure to have good posture; her failure to be obedient to tutors and others who, after all, were not her parents; her failure to be brave; her failure to be fearless.

Smith said, "Souvestre emancipated this bruised adolescent through the classroom, conversation, travel, and affirmation. Souvestre taught her how to think and, more important, valued what Eleanor thought. Allenswood offered Eleanor her first positive socialization with girls her age, and she became, as her cousin Corinne Robinson discovered, the most popular girl in the school, 'beloved by everybody.'"[26]

Marie Souvestre, the founder of the Allenswood School in Wimbledon, where Eleanor studied for three years. Eleanor kept her photo on her desk throughout her life. Courtesy of FDR Library.

"Souvestre helped emancipate Eleanor spiritually. The nurture her mother, grandmother, and aunts could not give, Souvestre had generously lavished. 'Whatever I have become since,' Eleanor confidently reminisced, 'had its seeds in those three years of contact with a liberal mind and a strong personality.'"[27]

In Christian mysticism, the third person of the Holy Trinity is often described as a mirror. The Holy Spirit shows you yourself. Clearly, Marie Souvestre held a mirror to Eleanor, even assuring her that beauty was more than personal appearance. Eleanor's description of history instruction at Allenswood reveals the newfound confidence this mirroring provided:

> The English girls were apt to remember what she had said and repeat it in their papers. I can still see her, as one of the girls was reading her paper aloud, standing over her with a long ruler in her hand, taking away the paper, and tearing it up.
>
> "You are giving me back what I gave you," she said, "and it does not interest me. You have not sifted it through your own intelligence. Why was your mind given you but to think things out for yourself?"
>
> It became a challenge for me to think about all the different sides of a situation and try to find new points that Mlle. Souvestre had not covered, points that had not even been covered in our books. It was rather exciting to have these questions come to mind as I read and I can remember now how pleased I was when she would ask me to leave my paper with her and later return it with the comment, "Well thought out, but have you forgotten this or that point?"
>
> That was an imaginative method of education and most valuable.[28]

Eleanor would honor Souvestre's memory for the rest of her life, keeping her picture on her desk and carrying her letters, along with her father's, in her purse. "Souvestre's spirited teaching shaped Eleanor's teaching at Todhunter School (1928–32). Blanche Wiesen Cook assesses a beloved teacher's lasting influence: 'Eleanor Roosevelt never turned away from the memory of Marie Souvestre. Her influence and spirit burned deeply within ER, and her teachings continually pointed in the direction of what was possible by way of independence, self-fulfillment, public activity, and human understanding.'"[29]

There was one problem though. Marie Souvestre was an atheist.

Eleanor took to heart her teacher's encouragement to think for herself and to disagree, when necessary. Eleanor challenged Souvestre's atheism directly and held her own in the spirited debates that followed. Her grandson said it may be the only matter on which they disagreed. He noted she told her friend William Turner Levy that Souvestre "simply refused to acknowledge that she was following standards she hadn't invented. She was following love, as we all must, and that is to follow God."[30]

Shortly after FDR was elected president, Eleanor wrote an essay entitled "What Religion Means to Me." In it she discussed Souvestre's views that Christians did good in hope of reward in the afterlife, suggesting that the "only people of real virtue were those who believed that there was no future life, but who wished to help those around them . . . purely through an interest in their fellow human beings and a desire to see right triumph just because it was right."

In Eleanor's view, no human could accurately judge the goodness of a deed or the purity of motivation. That is why, she said, all of us "crave the belief in some power greater than ourselves and beyond our understanding" because only such a power could effectively judge "what a human soul has achieved."[31]

The record does not indicate whether Eleanor maintained her churchgoing habits at Allenswood, but it is unlikely that she fell away from what had been a lifelong practice both before and after her time at school. Maintaining it would have been easy to do. There were several Church of England parishes in Wimbledon, the closest being about a six-minute walk from the campus. St. Paul's, Wimbledon Parkside, had strong ties to the Oxford movement, which had so profoundly affected Eleanor's first rector. It would have been a comfortable fit.

She showed no signs of breaking with the church, even temporarily. After Christmas in London with her Aunt Tissie, she traveled to Shropshire, where she spent a few days with the family of the rector of the church in Bridgenorth. The rector's wife was an American who was related to Eleanor by marriage. "She was Douglas Robinson's sister and held closely to her American ties, so that, though I could only be considered a connection by marriage, I was made to feel like a real relative and taken into the family and treated like one of the children. I enjoyed every minute of that visit, which was my first glimpse of English family life."[32] That summer Aunt Tissie took her to see the Passion Play at Oberammergau.

Joseph Lash has suggested that Souvestre was really an agnostic who said she was an atheist to be provocative. Eleanor tested the waters. The following Christmas, teacher and student vacationed in Florence. Souvestre joined Eleanor for midnight mass.

On a visit to Marseilles, they visited "a little church where offerings were made to the Blessed Virgin for the preservation of those at sea. There is a shrine in this church where people have prayed for the granting of some particular wishes, the crippled have hung their crutches there, and people have made offerings of gold and silver and jewels."[33]

REASSESSING GRANDMA

All her biographers agree that Mlle. Souvestre was largely responsible for Eleanor's emergence from the cocoon. But was there anything of value in that long period of dormancy that preceded the "miracle" at Allenswood?

In attempting to understand how a child overcomes a great difficulty such as the loss of a parent, a disability of some kind, great poverty, or some other deprivation that other children do not have, it is helpful to ask the question: "What went right in childhood?" Was there an adult who filled the void or a role model who provided inspiration? Was there a source of hope or at least a reason for it? Was there anything the child could count on?

While many of Eleanor's biographers conclude that the rigors of life with Grandmother Hall were oppressive, at least three things came of it that surely had positive value. The first was a kind of "moral deposit," and the second was the realization of a gift. The third was stability.

Mary Hall created a daily routine of Bible reading and formal household prayer. This routine required Eleanor, her brother, and those of her aunts and uncles who were still living at home to memorize Bible verses and to be drilled on them. Memorizing something is not the worst thing a child can be asked to do, but it is often excoriated as pointless or tedious, an attempt to control or possibly prevent independent thought. Yet the task of memorization can become a game, a challenge that the youngster may actually enjoy. It can also yield a sense of mastery that can be applied to other endeavors. In this latter aspect, instead of oppression it can actually be a possibility-expanding liberation.

It appears that Eleanor eventually came to see such discipline as a kind of liberation. In 1963 she wrote, "Democracy requires both discipline and hard work. It is not easy for individuals to govern themselves. . . . It is one thing to gain freedom, but no one can give you the right to self-government. This you must earn for yourself by long discipline."[34]

In the case of Eleanor's particular routine, this activity also had the desirable effect of providing content to the formation of her conscience. She was not simply admonished to be "good." She was absorbing stories and concepts that created a kind of moral savings account she would draw on for the rest of her life. Wisdom sayings or Bible verses lodged deep and reliably in memory, like the words of a favorite song or poem, can seemingly appear out of nowhere at any time. They can appear in times of trouble, to be sure, but also to interpret events, even to express joy. Eleanor, in short, was given a lot to draw on.

The second of Grandmother Hall's requirements was that Eleanor instruct her younger brother and the coachman's daughter in the very same arts of memorizing verses and learning hymns and the Prayer Book catechism. While seen as oppressive by some, the requirement nonetheless built on the mastery she had experienced while also showing her that she could teach the same skill to others. In some small way, these exercises gave her a rudimentary confidence that would expand to impressive dimensions as an adult. They also gave her the experience of being a teacher, a role she would play in adulthood in several different guises—as an instructor at the Rivington Street Settlement, as vice principal of the Todhunter School, and as a widely read columnist and sought-after public speaker.

These domestic routines provided an additional benefit to Eleanor. They had the effect, perhaps were *designed* to have the effect, of reinforcing and anticipating what she would experience in the Sunday liturgy at church. Over the course of a lifetime, participation in the kind of liturgical worship the Episcopal Church has historically provided greatly expands the "deposit" of the faith and fine-tunes the conscience. Constant recitation of psalms, an annual cycle of seasons with repetitive observances of various feasts and fasts, rhyming hymnody, beautiful visual stimulation—all combine to enable the participant to absorb enduring truths. Preaching, which seeks to interpret these various elements, can move these truths from the subliminal to the conscious realm, providing a fortification for the periods of great doubt, both cosmic and personal, that are sure to come. And it can provide concrete examples of how to apply these truths in day-to-day life.

To be sure, Mrs. Hall had some other "beliefs" that affected Eleanor's life, but they were not of a religious nature. "She believed that a daily cold sponge bath kept one from catching cold," Eleanor recalled, "and I took cold sponge baths for years. She believed that if I caught cold or had a headache it was a result of my own foolishness and that I should be expected to keep myself in good health. All this was spartan treatment and it was, I think, carried to excess, but I must confess that even today I feel that I am responsible for using common sense in keeping myself in good health."[35]

While a cold sponge bath may sound harsh and unnecessarily unpleasant to modern ears, the Roosevelt side of the family subscribed to similar views. Her grandfather, Theodore Roosevelt Sr., had prescribed a rigorous outdoor life and Spartan discipline as a remedy for young Teddy's asthma and other bodily infirmities. Following Elliott's fainting episodes at St. Paul's, the elder Roosevelt prescribed the same for his younger son. At the age of sixteen, Eleanor's father was sent to Fort McKavett, in the Texas hill country, where the family was acquainted with many of the officers. "This may seem to have been an inappropriate treatment for a medical ailment," Joseph Lash observed, "but in wealthy families of that era travel was the standard prescription for illnesses, nervous disorders, and unhappy love affairs." He said Elliott had "an unusual ability to fit into any situation and a zest for adventure . . . and without complaint made the transition from the comfortable, closed, and protected life of New York society to the rough equalitarianism of the frontier."[36]

His daughter, having experienced rigorous disciplines of her own, would develop a similar zest for adventure, leading her to opine late in life that the "purpose of life is to live it, to taste experience to the utmost, to reach out eagerly and without fear for newer and richer experiences."[37] Having a turn at the controls of Amelia Earhart's airplane and going to the front lines in the Guadalcanal are only two examples of her many adventures.

All of the routine disciplines—the memorizations, the liturgical worship, the cold baths—were a stable part of Eleanor's life even in the worst of times. It may be the answer to the questions so many historians ask about her. How did she do it? How did she overcome the hardships she faced? Clearly, she had a foundation of stability, and she learned how to create it for herself in adult life.

The importance of stability cannot be underestimated. As much as we desire freedom, there can be no freedom without an underlying stability. Even the most avant-garde, freewheeling dance requires a stable platform beneath the feet of the dancers. The most energetic entrepreneur still needs law, honest bankers, and reliable business norms. Faithful Fido still needs to be fed *every* night. Thus, a repetitive, predictable routine in the home might have been more valuable than young Eleanor realized. Time spent with her father, however desirable and comforting, was nonetheless irregular and unpredictable. The steady, possibly boring, routine of her early adolescence created a zone of stability, reinforced by the church's liturgy, enabling Eleanor to realize in her own life one of the overarching values of Anglicanism.

The Benedictine monks who developed Christianity in England in the fifth century did not take the vows of poverty, chastity, and obedience associated with the monastic orders that developed later on the continent. Instead, the Benedictines vowed *stability*, *obedience*, and *conversion of life*. As the American heir of the Church of England, the Episcopal Church and its religious orders have maintained Anglicanism's emphasis on stability. Most of the religious orders in the American church are Benedictine.

The word "stability" itself has more than one meaning, and it shows up in more than one way in the life and legacy of Eleanor Roosevelt. Most often we associate the term with the quality of *being* "stable" or "steady" (from the Latin *stabilis*—to stand firm). In this sense it implies "not easily moved or thrown off balance," firm in character, purpose, and resolution. Anyone who knew Eleanor would describe her as "firm in character, purpose, and resolution."

Another meaning is the capacity to regain equilibrium, as in a ship that rocks from port to starboard but stays afloat and moves forward. This meaning is visible in the Episcopal Church's commitment to "both . . . and" as opposed to "either . . . or." Critics of the church (including some Episcopalians) say it leads to a wishy-washy, noncommittal "middle of the road-ism," but apologists for the church prefer the term *via media*, an intentional valuing of the middle way, a considered appreciation of balance. This affirmative characterization reflects both the Thomistic and Aristotelian notion that truth and virtue lie in the tension between the polarities, what both philosophers called the "Golden Mean," the sweet spot between the extremes.

In the monastic tradition, the term also incorporates the idea of *place*. Benedictine monks vow to remain in the same monastery for life. They, of course, do their work and live out much of their lives in many different places all over the world, but they always return to the motherhouse. In 1926, FDR purchased land adjacent to his Springwood estate and gave it to Eleanor to build the cottage known as Val-Kill. Eleanor described the charming Dutch Colonial cottage as her first real home of her own. Despite her extensive travels, especially in her work on behalf of the United Nations, she would return to Val-Kill whenever she could. It served the same restorative and regenerative purposes as the monk's return to the motherhouse.

Eleanor knew that stability could not be taken for granted. The upheavals of her childhood had surely taught her that. But as a young adult, her participation in the Women's Trade Union League introduced her to the inherent *in*stability of the industrial system. The irregularity and low pay of factory work threatened the stability of the home, a home which could easily be lost with a sudden loss of income. Frequent, often catastrophic, workplace accidents incapacitated and sometimes permanently disabled the breadwinner, further destabilizing the family.

In the years immediately after her debut to society, Eleanor joined the Junior League for the Promotion of Settlement Movements, founded by her friend, fellow New York Episcopalian Mary Harriman. Settlement houses trace their origins to the Benedictine idea of blossoming in place. Toynbee Hall, the model for Chicago's famous Hull House, was a mission project of a London parish of the Church of England. Ellen Gates Starr, Jane Addams partner and cofounder, joined the Episcopal Church and embraced the Anglo-Catholic tradition. Another Anglo-Catholic, Wellesley professor Vida Scudder, organized the College Settlement Association, which sought to develop settlement houses in all the big cities of the United States. As a young woman, Eleanor would teach calisthenics at the association's Rivington Street Settlement, and she would take her fiancé, Franklin, to visit the settlement and the tenements where the clientele lived.

In her book *Seeking God: The Way of St. Benedict*, the noted scholar of monasticism Esther de Waal writes:

> Stability says there must be no evasion; instead attend to the real, to the real necessity however uncomfortable that might be. Stability brings us from a feeling of alienation, perhaps from the escape into fantasy and daydreaming, into the state of reality. It will not allow us to evade the inner truth of whatever it is that we

> have to do, however dreary and boring and apparently unfruitful that may seem. It involves listening . . . to the particular demands of whatever this task and this moment in time is asking; no more and no less.[38]

In her book *You Learn by Living*, Eleanor addressed the question of how she maintained such a heavy schedule throughout her life. She said it required first getting herself into a completely calm state and then giving the next task her undivided attention. Although she did not use the term "centering," many people today would recognize the meditative practice she describes. It was as if she found it necessary to first touch the stable earth before soaring off into the adventures of the day. Stability provided her restless heart with the ability to focus her attention and channel her energy. It gave her heart the freedom to dance.

CHAPTER THREE

ELEANOR AND THE RELIGIOUS CULTURE OF NEW YORK

No discussion of the religious formation of Eleanor Roosevelt would be complete without an exploration of the larger community of which her multiple parishes were a part. Many of the concerns of this larger community became concerns for Eleanor too, and she addressed them in myriad ways throughout her life. As noted in chapter one, before her marriage, Eleanor already had ties to three parishes in the Diocese of New York: Calvary, where she was baptized; Incarnation, where she was confirmed; and St. Paul's, Tivoli, where she spent her summers. When she married, she added St. James', Hyde Park, to her "church homes." When she lived on her own in Greenwich Village after her husband's death, she would worship at St. Luke-in-the-Fields. Eleanor Roosevelt essentially lived out her entire life in the Diocese of New York. Even during her years in Albany and Washington, D.C., she maintained her ties, especially with St. James', Hyde Park, where she worshipped on her returns to Springwood and Val-Kill.

Eleanor was born at a time when New York was eclipsing Boston as the cultural and intellectual center of the nation. For more than one hundred fifty years, the old Puritan-inspired New England Theology had held sway over much of the country, informing its political philosophies as well as its literary output and other cultural patterns. Jonathan Edwards, author of *Sinners in the Hands of an Angry God,* set the tone for this theological perspective. By the late nineteenth century, though, the New England Theology was giving way to a more Catholic-minded New York Theology with a kinder view of human nature and a less restrictive understanding of community. It would be a progenitor of the ecumenism of the century to come. The Diocese of New York played a leadership role in fostering a religious culture that emphasized community service and generosity of spirit as opposed to personal prudence and social discipline.

In terms of the broader culture, the theater, which was still being censored or outright banned in Boston, was flourishing on the New York stage. The dramatic character of liturgy in the city's Episcopal and Roman Catholic churches was both a generator and a magnet for the city's large theater community. Accordingly, the Reverend Walter Edmund Bentley organized the Actors' Church Alliance in 1899, with Eleanor's bishop, Henry Codman Potter, serving as the first president. The organization later gave birth to the Episcopal Actors Guild, the Catholic Actors Guild, and the Jewish Actors Guild.

Eleanor's grounding in a liturgical tradition may have contributed to her own attraction to the theater. At the tender age of thirteen, she was given money to go to a church fair but spent the money instead on a ticket for *Tess of the d'Urbervilles.* Her young aunts had seen it but told Eleanor she was too young.[1] She decided to see for herself. Throughout her adult years, she went to the theater whenever her busy schedule would permit, often taking friends or guests along.

Another aspect of the broader culture was also relevant to religious life in New York. Paris would soon pass the torch to New York as the world center of the fine arts. Painting, sculpture, and stained glass, as noted earlier, were all a prominent part of Eleanor's church life. The work of both aspiring and well-known artists adorned not just the Church of the Incarnation, but Episcopal and Catholic churches throughout the city, in stark contrast to the normative patterns of New England.

The city would become the center of the publishing industry and the incubator of the nascent film, radio, and ultimately television industries. Eleanor loved to read as a child and would be a widely published author over the course of her life. Many of the preachers who filled the pulpits of her parish churches were already or soon-to-be published authors, a logical development for thought leaders in what would become the communications capital of the world.

The Archdiocese of New York was already the nation's largest Roman Catholic diocese at the time Eleanor was born. By the time she was a young adult, New York would also be home to the world's largest Jewish community. At the same time, the Episcopal Church and many other mainline denominations would locate their national headquarters in New York, giving the city an ecumenical flavor unmatched anywhere in the country. To understand the practical implications of this cultural and theological shift, it is helpful to look in on an earlier time.

The year was 1891. Eleanor was not quite seven years old and was most likely not present at this particular gathering, but it tells us a good deal about the self-understanding of the church of her baptism and the direction her own life would ultimately take.

The setting was old Trinity Church, sturdily enthroned on the highest point overlooking Wall Street. A processional cross led the choir and vested clergy down the center aisle. Processions themselves, especially those led by a cross, were rare enough in US Protestantism in those days, but this one pushed the envelope beyond the latent fears of resurgent royalism that haunted nineteenth-century America. Behind the cross, a black man carried a *red* flag. This was *not* a liturgical banner of Pentecost, although Vida Scudder, the Christian socialist professor from Wellesley, assures us that the connection is clear. No, this was *the* red flag, the one that would inspire—and terrify—the century to come.

Immediately behind him, a white man carried that other inspiring and terrifying flag—the Stars and Stripes. The occasion was the second in a series of Labor Sunday masses promoted by the Church Association for the Advancement of the Interests of Labor, popularly known by the acronym CAIL. Bishop Potter had been one of the founders of CAIL and its vice president. His prestigious presence that day offered both an imprimatur and a guarantee of citywide attention. Trade union officials, mostly Irish Catholics, marched in procession, and the rank and file filled the pews to overflowing, according to Scudder.[2]

To those for whom the wealth and prestige of Trinity Church seemed to be its defining characteristics, this warm embrace of a social movement that was racially, ethnically, religiously, and economically diverse must have been a shock. As an adult, Eleanor would be a champion of all of the groups represented at that Labor Sunday mass. Was her advocacy born of mysteriously acquired *political* convictions, or was she giving voice to values embedded in her religious community? If the latter, then it is legitimate to ask why such values were there to begin with?

A THEOLOGICAL ALLIANCE BETWEEN RICH AND POOR?

What was the basis of an alliance between the diocese and the labor movement? Was it noblesse oblige? Paternalism?

Appeasement of the restless masses? Veiled exploitation? Enlightened self-interest? Or an early form of radical chic?

Many commentators would pick one or more of the above. But could it have been *theological*? If we are to understand Eleanor's embrace of the labor movement and her husband's support of her commitments, serious attention must be given to the theological question. Does the social location of the richest and the poorest in society give rise to an understanding of God that might be different from that of people in the middle? The answer emerges when the relevance of *circumstance* is compared to the relevance of *individual effort*. People with inherited wealth, like the Roosevelts, know they did not earn it no matter how worthy of it they may think themselves. Likewise, people born into poverty know they did not create their deprivation despite what the advocates of moral improvement might say. Both groups are likely to view their situation as "a given"—something that came to them as a function of fate, some would say, or by the grace of God, according to others.

Eleanor herself came from several generations of inherited wealth on both sides of her family. From an early age, she was well-aware that her economic circumstances as well as those of the unfortunate ones she learned to care about had virtually nothing to do with individual choice or effort.

This understanding of heredity and circumstance was, of course, very different from the perspective of people between those extremes. For the middle classes, individual effort, talent, and merit are what matter in the end. And their life experience, especially in the world of business, tends to validate that view. Not enough hard work, and they may be worse off than when they started out. A little bit more, and they may be better off by far.

Similar differences in perception attach to agrarian versus urban settings. In the agrarian context, no matter how much planting and cultivation is done, material success still has a lot to do with the wind and the rain and the birds and the bees. In the urban world of commerce and industry, though, shrewd calculation, effective planning, prudent use of resources, and correct anticipation of supply and demand carry the day. Judgment, rather than fate, is what really matters.

With these distinctions in mind, it is not difficult to see why, in the English Civil War, both the landed aristocracy and the peasantry who farmed the estates clung to a Catholic worldview that emphasized divine agency, thanksgiving, and celebration, while the urban mercantile classes were drawn to a Calvinist view that emphasized discipline, judgment, and anticipation? *Grace* and *hereditary birthright* on the one hand versus *personal righteousness* and *meritocracy* on the other.

Of course by 1891 it is doubtful that anyone at CAIL's Labor Sunday mass was thinking of the political alignments of the English Civil War, although historian Kevin Phillips asserts that the Cavalier-Roundhead cleavage is traceable through Anglo-American politics right up to the close of the nineteenth century.[3] In fact, it continues to the present day with Democrats carrying the banner for social responsibility and Republicans standing the ground for economic freedom. Eleanor, consistent with both her social and theological heritage, would grow up to embody social responsibility.

Despite the persistence of the core cleavage Phillips identifies, it is important to note that Trinity Church, from its founding, had always had a handsome share of the urban merchant class in its membership. At the time of the American Revolution, even though Trinity's rector fled to Nova Scotia, several Trinity members, such as John Jay and Alexander Hamilton, would become architects of the young republic. The historical pattern, therefore, does not replicate itself with scientific precision. Yet when viewed through an institutional lens, the socioeconomic skeleton of the old Cavalier alliance is still visible. Trinity Church was (and still is) a landed aristocrat. In 1705, Queen Anne endowed Trinity with a "glebe"—a farm to generate revenue for the church. Trinity's glebe stretched from nearby Fulton Street to Christopher Street in present-day Greenwich Village. Over time, farming gave way to real estate development. To this very day, a number of Wall Street skyscrapers pay ground rents to this parish of the Episcopal Church.

The demographic lens yields similar results. The urban working classes were (and still are) the heirs of the rural peasantry, displaced by cash crops and driven to the cities for survival. And just as staunchly Catholic Irish peasants once made common cause with the otherwise obnoxious Anglican establishment in their efforts to resist Oliver

Cromwell's advances in Ireland during the English Civil War, by the 1890s their emigrant descendants were the backbone of New York's labor movement. Hence, the not-so-strange participation of loyal Irish Catholics in a Labor Sunday liturgy straight out of the Book of Common Prayer.

It was not Trinity Church but rather Trinity's *tenants* who had turned Wall Street into the capital of capitalism. Trinity was the Lord of the Manor. It would have received rents from the estate whether it had continued as farmland or had been developed for residential housing or defense fortifications. Trinity's wealth, then, was not earned. It was literally "a given," just like Eleanor's wealth and the poverty of the people she and the church sought to help.

Although the diocese itself was not created until 1785 when post-revolutionary disestablishment forced Church of England congregations to reorganize themselves into what we now know as the Episcopal Church, the foundations of a New York theology were visible from the earliest days of English rule.

As a proprietary colony owned by the Dutch West India Company, the province of New Netherlands practiced a form of religious toleration that allowed residents to worship in their homes according to any tradition, but only the Dutch Reformed Church could erect buildings and conduct public worship. Quakers, Lutherans, and other Christians resided in the colony, and there was also a small Jewish community. This arrangement meant that even with an official church, there was a high degree of religious pluralism in the colony from the very beginning.

Although Eleanor's Livingston forbears appear to have been Episcopalians from the earliest days of British settlement, the Roosevelts, as noted earlier, began their life in the New World as part of the Dutch Reformed Church. Following the mostly peaceful surrender of the colony to England under very favorable terms to the Dutch inhabitants in 1664, the Church of England would become the established church for the newly designated colony of New York, and the church's emphasis on grace and providence would lay the foundations for the New York Theology that would be fully developed by the time of Eleanor's birth.

THE GOD OF GRACE VS. THE GOD OF JUDGMENT

Unlike the Puritan vision for New England, New York was not intended to be a "city on a hill" as John Winthrop envisioned the Massachusetts Bay Colony.[4] It was not conceptualized as a reformed and purer version of England. Instead, it was to be an extension of gritty, hustling metropolitan London, a crown colony named for the Duke of York who would one day be King James II. It would not be a community of the "elect," the "regenerate," the "convinced," or the "converted." Essentially, it would be a community of whoever showed up. No need for witch trials, as in Salem, or other tests of doctrinal purity.

As in the "mother country," the Church of England in New York would be responsible for the well-being of the *whole* community, whether they were church members or not. The joint monarchs William and Mary said as much in the charter they granted to Trinity in 1697. Their successor, Queen Anne, would assure that the parish had the means to do so. The revenues from her generous grant enabled the parish to found or substantially endow many of the city's leading institutions, including King's College, now Columbia University.

While the American Revolution resulted in the disestablishment of the Church of England in New York, it did not result in a renunciation of the values the church advanced and that Eleanor inherited: a Catholic conception of community—broad, comprehensive, comfortable with internal diversity—and an emphasis on the affirming grace of God rather than his disapproving judgment. This emphasis was accompanied by an affirmative view of human nature uncharacteristic of most of the forms of Protestantism that entered this country during the colonial period. Human beings were basically good in this view. Sin was a function of human frailty, not of congenital rebelliousness or innate wickedness as implied by Calvin's concept of the "total depravity" of humankind.

With the founding of the republic, New York State became the first North American polity to offer full citizenship to Jews. By 1806, Roman Catholics enjoyed the same status. By the time of Eleanor's birth, the majority of New York City residents would be Roman Catholic, with Jews and Episcopalians the second and third largest groups, respectively. The shared values of these three traditions carried over into the city's civic and political life. All of the city's twentieth-century mayors would come from one of these three groups.

This sociological configuration was a significant factor in the development of the New York Theology. Anglicanism had been a minority tradition even when it was official, but now with the growth of the Catholic and Jewish population, the majority of New Yorkers shared Anglicanism's affirmative view of human nature and its comfort with diversity. Both the Catholic Church in New York and the Jewish community were multiethnic and multilingual, and as we shall see momentarily, so was the Episcopal Church in New York. Unlike most forms of Protestantism, all three traditions shared an Aristotelian, i.e., philosophically realist, worldview. All three emphasized social *provision* rather than social *discipline*. And all three were the primary providers of services to the city's immigrant population. Catholic and Jewish organizations had a major role born of obvious necessity: Most of the immigrants were either Catholic or Jewish. Episcopalians had their historic assignment of social *duty* and, quite frankly, the historic money that came with it.

Despite many legal challenges over the years, Trinity managed to retain its pre-Revolutionary endowments, and the mother church of the Diocese of New York would continue to found hospitals, schools, and social service agencies as well as chapels, missions, and parishes just as it had done in the colonial period. Indeed, Trinity had called on Eleanor's father to help expand this work.

By Eleanor's time, Trinity was underwriting both national and international programs as well as the more immediate needs of New York City and the diocese. Eleanor's interests and commitments would eventually expand along the same lines. Her work with poor children at the Rivington Street Settlement and her work in the Women's Trade Union League are examples that we will explore more fully in the next chapter. Eventually she would be a member of both the Newspaper Guild (for her own work) and the United Autoworkers (in solidarity). Her theological outlook almost perfectly embodied the tenets of the New York Theology and its emphasis on the abundant God of grace rather than the angry God of judgment.

THE LABOR CONNECTION

The day Eleanor was born, a priest from the Diocese of New York was the keynote speaker at a church gathering in Detroit called to address the question: "Is Our Civilization Just to Workingmen?" The Reverend Richard Heber Newton of All Souls, New York City, did not think it was.

"Labor's complaint is poverty," he said. "Poverty is the fault neither of the laborer nor of nature. The state crosses the path of the working man and prevents him from making a fair fight. Labor fails to get favorable legislation; capital secures all it asks."[5] In Newton's day, the Supreme Court of the United States regularly invalidated state attempts to regulate working conditions on the grounds that such regulations constrained the rights of property owners and investors and infringed on the workers' rights to freedom of contract. Even when legislatures attempted to guarantee more favorable conditions for workers, the Supreme Court "crossed their path," striking down any laws the states managed to pass. Newton's assertion that *circumstance* (the "system") rather than individual effort is responsible for poverty reflects the New York Theology. Writing on such topics as *The Morals of Trade* and *The Right and Wrong Uses of the Bible*, Newton often attracted criticism and accusations of heresy. But the bishop of New York stood by him.

Henry Codman Potter would be Eleanor's bishop until she turned twenty-four. Although New York had been historically understood as a "high church" diocese—placing a high value on tradition, the sacraments, and the historic three-fold ministry of bishops, priests, and deacons—Bishop Potter would be best described as "broad church," a term that was gaining currency in his day as people grew weary of the controversies associated with the rivalry between the high church and low church parties. The broad-church concept was that multiple viewpoints could coexist in the same church. One did not have to take sides. There could be diversity within a larger unity. A case in point was the creation of the Order of the Holy Cross to be an Episcopal monastic order for men. Bishop Potter was aware that some in the church opposed the revival of religious orders in the Anglican Communion, partly because they feared the orders would become potent sources of high church propaganda and partly because they felt the celibate life was an affront to the sanctity of marriage. Nonetheless, the Reverend James Otis Sargent Huntington had been doing solid work in the labor movement on the Lower East Side and was the principal organizer of CAIL. Thus, the good bishop presided at Father Huntington's life profession of vows about a month after Eleanor was born.[6] Despite discomfort in some quarters, the Order of the Holy Cross flourished. Twenty years later, it would open a monastery on the west bank of the Hudson, visible across the river from the Roosevelt estate at Hyde Park.

The term "broad church" could also be applied accurately to Eleanor, who as an adult sometimes worshiped on a regular basis in Anglo-Catholic strongholds, such as All Saints' Cathedral in Albany and St. Luke-in-the-Fields in Greenwich Village. Her paternal grandmother, Martha Bulloch Roosevelt, worshiped at the Church of the Transfiguration, popularly known as the Little Church Around the Corner. It was founded with the intention of creating a model parish of the Anglo-Catholic persuasion. Its founder, the Reverend George Houghton, had also made it a stop on the Underground Railroad. During the Civil War draft riots, a shocking number of free black New Yorkers were lynched in the streets, scapegoated as the cause of the war and the reason for the draft. Father Houghton was sheltering as many as he could in the church proper, but he needed more space. He asked Mrs. Roosevelt, the sister of two Confederate soldiers from a slaveholding family, if she would shelter some people in her commodious town house nearby. Although she never renounced her Confederate sympathies, she nonetheless did as her rector requested, illustrating how seriously the concept of "agreeing to disagree" was regarded in the church.

For Eleanor's part, we can see how this disposition of the church in her formative years built her capacity to learn about and genuinely respect people who were not only different from her but had come to different conclusions about what mattered in life. Based on her parochial affiliations, it appears that she was comfortable in both the more florid Anglo-Catholic settings as well as parishes that had fewer liturgical embellishments and thought of themselves as mainline Protestant.

The concept of diversity within unity was especially appropriate for the Diocese of New York. In some respects, diversity was its middle name. New York Anglicanism was internally diverse, almost from the very beginning. Significant numbers of Huguenot and Dutch Reformed New Yorkers had been, willingly and unwillingly, incorporated into the church at the time of its establishment. Early eighteenth-century work among the Iroquois and among African Americans added racial diversity. The development of Italian, Chinese, and German-speaking parishes had followed the founding of St. Ann's Church for the Deaf, which used American Sign Language. By the time Eleanor was six years old, the diocese could claim that Eucharist was celebrated every Sunday in nine different languages!

DON'T IRON WHILE THE STRIKE IS HOT

Because parishes like Eleanor's had developed so many ministries oriented toward the poor and working class, there was a remarkably acute awareness of labor concerns throughout the diocese. Even before he was a bishop, Henry Codman Potter had seen labor struggles close-up when he served as rector of St. John's in Troy, New York, early in his career. At the time, the cities of Troy and neighboring Cohoes directly across the river were a major center of the detachable collar industry, which made the Arrow Collar famous. Cluett Brothers and Company was the largest of fourteen collar manufacturers in the area. Manufacturing collars required large, industrial-scale laundries, which were staffed almost entirely by women. The work entailed a number of dangers, such as handling scalding hot water, harsh chemicals, and hot irons, to say nothing of heat so high the factories became known as "sweatshops." Serious burn injuries and heat exhaustion were common problems along with low pay.

In 1864, twenty-six-year-old Kate Mullany, the sole breadwinner for her widowed mother and younger sisters, formed the Collar Laundry Union of Troy, the first all-female labor union in the United States. In February of that year, she led a strike of three hundred women, which lasted five days. Although the employers insisted they could not meet the demand for higher wages, emboldened by Mullany's catchy slogan "Don't iron while the strike is hot," the union succeeded in winning a 25 percent increase in wages and improved working conditions. Part of the reason why the employers gave in is that the women's union enjoyed widespread community support as well as the technical and financial assistance of the all-male Troy Iron Molders Union No. 2.

Some fifty years before Eleanor was born, St. John's was already supporting causes that would become important to Eleanor. In 1831, it began providing financial support to a struggling African American parish in Fayetteville, North Carolina. Later, it would become the parish home of Emma Willard, the pioneering advocate of women's education, who founded the Troy Female Seminary, the first school for women's higher education in the United States. Despite this progressive pedigree, the strike undoubtedly posed a dilemma for the parish and its young rector. It was broadly supported in the wider community for which Potter, as a prominent clergyman, was expected to be a leader. Yet its ultimate target was the wealthy Cluett family who were prominent and generous members of the parish he headed. It is not clear how Potter responded in that situation, but the commitments he embraced over the next twenty years placed him squarely in the center of the quest for just and favorable working conditions. According to the lore of the diocese, the good bishop reportedly said, "If the church required me to work under the same conditions as New York's laboring masses, I'd go on strike too!"

Frances Perkins, FDR's secretary of labor and a devout churchwoman herself, said Bishop Potter was the first person she ever heard say "labor is not a commodity."[7] While he may not have originated the slogan that was widely used in the labor movement, it was nonetheless the concept that undergirded the understanding that Perkins, FDR, and their allies would embed in American labor law in the 1930s: A commodity can be repossessed if the purchaser does not pay for it. Labor cannot be recovered. Once expended it is gone. Therefore, the agreed upon wages must be fully paid within two weeks of performance. This was the same understanding that Eleanor would carry into her human rights work.

As he progressed toward becoming the bishop of New York, Potter steadily acquired a reputation as someone who could be on good terms with both capital and labor. By the time Eleanor was born, he had been appointed as chairman of CAIL's Council of Mediation and Arbitration, where he served with Columbia University president and future mayor of New York Seth Low and John Newton Bogart of the Typographical Union.[8] By the time Eleanor began her studies at Allenswood, her bishop had become a member of the Committee on Conciliation and Mediation of the National Civic Union. As part of this work, he would be a mediator of the strike against US Steel in 1901. He later told the men's club at Grace Church, where he had previously been the rector, that he believed in strikes, but that he also believed the day was coming when strikes would cease, because men would one day ask themselves in the presence of their differences, not what considerations of profit and dividends, but what considerations of justice and humanity are involved.[9] To be sure, that hopeful prophecy was not on the horizon.

Not all of the bishop's overtures to the working class were successful. One of his most clever and innovative efforts was a large-scale, publicly embarrassing failure.

THE SUBWAY TAVERN

In 1904, with much fanfare and public skepticism, Bishop Potter presided at the opening of the Subway Tavern, a venture to offer an alternative to the perceived exploitation of the working class. While many other denominations were urging the temperance movement toward full-scale prohibition, the Episcopal Church continued to favor moderation. The concept of the Subway Tavern was to create a working-class version of the many private clubs that dotted the city—a wholesome environment where alcoholic beverages could be enjoyed without being pressured to buy more, where decent food would be available. High-quality literature would be on hand for casual reading, and bartenders would be trained to monitor and guide patrons to responsible drinking. It was modeled on taverns in England created by Earl Grey "to disassociate immorality from the drinking habit," according to *The New York Times*.

Contrary to what many thought, the tavern was not actually located in the subway, which in fact would not start operations until a few months after the tavern opened. It was in an aboveground building on the corner of Bleecker and Mulberry Streets in Greenwich Village, where a handsome glass-covered subway entrance had been built.

Speaking to a large crowd of prominent citizens at the tavern's dedication on August 2, 1904, Bishop Potter said, "In the great cities we must make the home of the workingmen better, cleaner, and brighter. We must see that they have recreation, which takes men not away from but into closer relations with their families and children."

He concluded his remarks by telling of places in Europe "where men went with their wives and children to hear good music and to eat and drink according to their means." As if to put the final *imprimatur* on the venture, the ceremonies ended with the crowd singing the doxology.[10]

The Episcopal Church's preference for temperance rather than outright prohibition may be one of the few points on which Eleanor disagreed with her bishop. Knowing what alcohol did to her father and how it affected the two uncles she lived with, Eleanor had resolved to be a teetotaler and also became an advocate of prohibition.

Despite all the fanfare and the bishop's good intentions, the establishment was never a hit with the people it was intended to serve. It closed at the end of one year and was replaced by a conventional saloon.

JEWISH-CHRISTIAN RELATIONS

As noted earlier, by the time of Bishop Potter's tenure, New York City was home to the world's largest Jewish community, estimated to number one million or more. A small percentage had been there from Peter Stuyvesant's time, founding synagogues, educational institutions, and service organizations. They were also significant providers of support to New York's settlement houses. But the vast majority of New York's Jews were Yiddish-speaking immigrants from Eastern Europe.

Potter was well-acquainted with both segments. As a civic leader, he often worked in partnership with prominent Jews or the organizations they created. His work in the labor movement put him in constant touch with the Jewish poor, who were a large component of the garment industry. Early in his tenure as bishop, Potter began to engage in public dialogues with Jewish leaders intended to challenge negative stereotypes, and he encouraged his clergy to do likewise. The Reverend William Reed Huntington, rector of Grace Church, Broadway, where Potter had once served, expressed support by tolling the bell of Grace Church in solemn support of the Jewish procession moving up Broadway mourning the Russian pogroms of 1905. He and Potter both opposed efforts in the General Convention, the church's national governing body, to promote evangelization among the Jews.

Eleanor was twenty-four years old when her bishop died in 1908. Rabbi Joseph Silverman of Temple Emanu-El offered a eulogy at an interfaith memorial at the Cooper Union detailing Bishop Potter's warm relations with the Jewish community.[11] The warm relations Silverman cited were not just a one-way street. The Reverend William Berrian's "Historical Sketch of Trinity Church" notes seven

Jewish donors listed among the contributors to the construction of a steeple for the Wall Street edifice in 1711.[12] Two hundred years later, Jewish donors would also be among those who contributed to the construction of the Cathedral of St. John the Divine, another of Potter's major projects. To this day, a menorah is prominently displayed near the high altar.

The warm relationship continued under Potter's successor, the Right Reverend David Greer, bishop of New York from 1908 to 1919. Greer took it upon himself to learn Yiddish to better understand the immigrants in his midst. Several years later, the Reverend Frank Stanton Burns Gavin would join the faculty of the General Theological Seminary on Manhattan's West Side, thus influencing all the younger clergy assigned to work in Eleanor's various parishes. Gavin held a degree in Hebraic literature from Hebrew Union College in Cincinnati and was a university fellow in Semitic languages at Columbia, where he earned his PhD. He later did postdoctoral study in Semitic and early Christian literature at Harvard.

In his lectures and subsequent book entitled *The Jewish Antecedents of the Christian Sacraments*, Gavin maintained that Christian traditions represented a *development* of earlier Jewish traditions, not a departure from, or replacement for, them. The ancient Kiddush supper was the ancestor of the Holy Communion, he said. (This work, and several others, were translated into Hebrew and are found in the National Library of Israel, with an affirmative description of the author.) In his commentaries on the creeds he took pains to stress that it was the Romans, not the Jews, who put Jesus to death.

As early as 1934, Gavin had assailed "Hitler worship" in Germany, but he did not live long enough to see how tragically accurate his perceptions were. He was felled by pneumonia in 1938. But the diocese was well aware of what was happening. Just seven days after Franklin and Eleanor Roosevelt moved into the White House, their bishop (from 1921), the Reverend William Thomas Manning, attended an anti-Nazi rally in Madison Square Garden. A *New York Times* photo shows him seated next to the renowned Rabbi Stephen Wise of the Free Synagogue.

Eleanor had begun her work with Jewish children on the Lower East Side when she was only nineteen years old. Her life in the Diocese of New York had provided her with an affirmative moral theology of Jewish-Christian relations.

THE CATHEDRAL OF ST. JOHN THE DIVINE

As early as 1828, the Right Reverend John Henry Hobart met with New York City Mayor Philip Hone to discuss the possibility of building a cathedral for the city. Although Hone was a member of St. Mark's-in-the-Bowery, the point of the meeting was not that he was a prominent churchman. The point was that Hobart wanted a cathedral that would be at the center of the city's civic life. He was seeking the city's support for a "house of prayer for all people." The idea, however, did not gain traction until 1873 when a charter was obtained from New York State. When

Eleanor was eight years old, Bishop Potter laid the cornerstone. Seven years later, the first services were held in chapel crypt. By the middle of the twentieth century, while still a work in progress, it was regarded as the world's largest Gothic cathedral. It was assumed that such a large size would be needed for a cathedral that would host great public events in a great city.

The assumption proved prescient. In 1962, ten thousand people crowded into the nave to hear Adlai Stevenson deliver his eulogy for the most prominent daughter of the diocese, Eleanor Roosevelt.

CHAPTER FOUR

MAKING SOMETHING ELSE OF LIFE

"Forbid us to be satisfied with" what we make of life. . . ."This phrase from the prayer Eleanor adopted for her nightly discipline articulates a hope that seems to have been planted in her heart from an early age. It might have been kindled by the adventurous attitudes of her father or perhaps the heroic achievements of her Uncle Teddy. No doubt the powerlessness of her teenaged years frustrated her sense that there was supposed to be something more to life than what she was being shown. Then the experience of Allenswood rekindled that dwindling flame.

In 1902, Eleanor reluctantly returned to New York. Marie Souvestre had felt she would benefit from another year of study, which was what Eleanor actually wanted, but her grandmother insisted that the time had come for Eleanor to be "presented" to society as was the custom for all the young women in the Hall and Roosevelt families. Marie Souvestre had warned her not to become caught up in the social whirl. Eleanor took the advice to heart, dreading almost every aspect of her "debut" and its aftermath.

Upon returning to New York, Eleanor spent the summer in Maine at Northeast Harbor, most likely worshipping at St. Mary's-by-the-Sea, which had only recently been built after several years of worshiping in a timber chapel. That December, she would make her formal debut to society. By all accounts, she was a "successful" debutante. While still haunted perhaps by the childhood notion that she was an "ugly duckling," she had become reasonably attractive as she matured. Described by one biographer as "tall and willowy" with "long golden hair swept back from her face and caught in a braid in the back," her slim figure was perfect for the Gibson Girl fashions of the day, which featured long-sleeved shirtwaists with slim ankle-length skirts.[1] She received and accepted the requisite invitations, often making perfunctory appearances and leaving early. Her restless spirit chafed at the endless round of luncheons, theater parties, and balls.

With her church's emphasis on social mission and economic justice in all the ways she encountered it—parish affiliations, family involvements, the widely publicized pronouncements of her bishop and his cathedral deans—Eleanor already had a strong sense of what kinds of things needed to be done. Her experience at Allenswood had developed her confidence and yielded a sense of her own

The reluctant debutante, Eleanor decided to minimize the social whirl and concentrate on work among the poor. Courtesy of FDR Library.

capabilities. She would not be satisfied with what had been made of her life so far.

It is not surprising that she chose to invest her time and energy in the world of settlement house work, tenement investigations, and labor advocacy. In terms of the moral/ecclesiastical universe she inhabited, she had been groomed for it from birth, but she had been in a state of suspended animation in the five years between her father's death and her enrollment at Allenswood.

While historians rightly credit Marie Souvestre with persuading Eleanor of her capabilities, a key factor in her growing sense of confidence was a deeply rooted sense that she was right about the things that actually mattered in life. Her church had continually lifted up public service and advocacy for the forgotten as moral ideals. It is a mistake to suggest that she "overcame" her religious heritage. In fact, she *fulfilled* it, first in her native city, then for the nation as a whole, and finally for the whole world. What other path could she have chosen that would have been more logical? What work of lesser scope would have been more satisfying?

She was eager to get to work on things that mattered. She resolved to make something else of her life. Her friend, Mary Harriman, a student at Barnard College, had just the solution to fill the bill.

Mary was the granddaughter of an impoverished Episcopal priest, the Reverend Orlando Harriman Jr., but she had had the good fortune to be born to Orlando's enterprising son, Edward, later known as railroad tycoon E. H. Harriman, and his equally enterprising wife, Mary Averell Harriman. Although the Harrimans had a chapel in their country home at Arden and were members of both St. John's, Arden, and St. Thomas, Fifth Avenue, Mary felt that working through the church was too sectarian and hospital work too limited in scope. Her concept would be to organize young women from all religious backgrounds to go into the settlement houses and do frontline social work among the needy. Thus, in 1901 at the age of nineteen, Mary organized the Junior League for the Promotion of Settlement Movements. Within ten years, the League had chapters throughout the United States. At the end of twenty, it had become an international organization.

Mary was something of an organizational genius, and she was undoubtedly an important role model for Eleanor, whose newfound confidence was still frail. Over the years of their friendship, Eleanor would develop similar organizational and time management skills.

Mary's success in organizing eighty young women and training them for social work while she was still a student was just the beginning. She would go on to organize agricultural cooperatives and to manage the family's Arden estate, which had six hundred employees. After World War I, she converted New York City's civil defense councils into advocates for parks and playgrounds, housing and transit improvement, and lower utility bills. When she moved to Washington at the beginning of the New Deal, she created the magazine we know today as *Newsweek* and organized the Consumer Advisory Board for the National Recovery Administration (NRA). She also joined St. Thomas', Dupont Circle, where Eleanor and Franklin worshipped during their Washington years.

While some of this genius may have been innate talent, Mary had stellar role models in her parents. Her father had involved her in both business and philanthropic activities

Mary Harriman (Rumsey), founder of the Junior League, had encouraged Eleanor to begin settlement house work. The two remained lifelong friends. Wikicommons.

from an early age. When she was seventeen, she accompanied him on a none-too-sentimental journey "countin' every mile of railroad track" in the Harriman demesne. Riding in a special car pushed ahead of a slow-moving locomotive, Mary and her father could see every bridge and crosstie of their five-thousand-mile journey, along with a backyard glimpse of the America that postcards rarely immortalize.[2]

Beyond this, Mary had also whiled away the hours with "Siberian Eskimos, drunken whalers, and down-and-out gold prospectors" as a participant in the legendary Harriman Expedition of 1899. What began as a doctor-ordered vacation cruise for her father grew into epic proportions when C. Hart Merriman, head of the US Biological Survey, was asked to select scientists from varied disciplines to join the trip to document the flora and fauna of the previously uncharted coast of Alaska. Notables such as John Muir, founder of the Sierra Club, and George Bird Grinnell, founder of the Audubon Society, and best-selling nature writer John Burroughs, were among the 126 passengers and crew. Lasting two months, the expedition returned with one hundred trunks of specimens and five thousand photographs and hand illustrations, which fueled a ten-year-long project to digest the new data.[3] But Mary's father was not just a man of science and industry. Like Eleanor's father and grandfather, he had a deep concern for the plight of the city's underprivileged boys. He is credited with founding the nation's first club for such boys on Manhattan's Lower East Side.

"Tycoonship," if there can be such a word, seems to have run in the family. Mary's mother handily took over the railroad after her husband died. And she readily applied her business acumen to philanthropic ventures as well, founding the Training School for Public Service, which later became the National Institute of Public Administration; establishing the Harriman Fund for Orthopaedics at the Yale School of Medicine; endowing a forestry chair at Yale; and, at her daughter's urging, creating the Eugenics Records Office at Cold Spring Harbor, Long Island, to study the relationship of heredity and mental deficiency. Mrs. Harriman served on the national board of the American Red Cross and was an active supporter of the visual and performing arts, founding the American Orchestral Society and financing the 1925 Tri-National Exhibition of Contemporary Art.[4]

THE COLLEGE SETTLEMENT

Eleanor could not have associated with a better example of a debutant who made something else of her life. As a Junior Leaguer, Eleanor's first work would be at the College Settlement Association's Rivington Street Settlement. One of the founders of the association was Vida Scudder, the Wellesley professor noted in the previous chapter, who would also be a founder of the Women's Trade Union League, which would later be another of Eleanor's interests

Located two blocks south of Houston Street on the Lower East Side, the people of the neighborhood were predominantly immigrant Jews. Eleanor recalled that the "dirty streets, crowded with foreign-born people, filled me with terror, and I often waited on a corner for a [street] car, watching with a great deal of trepidation, men come out of the saloons or shabby hotels nearby."[5] Yet this fear did not stop her. She said working with the children had become enormously important to her and a source of great satisfaction.

She taught calisthenics and fancy dancing. For a young woman who had suffered curvature of the spine as a child, it is not difficult to see why she understood the importance of her work. Curvature was a major problem for children who worked in the garment industry. Boys, in particular, were expected to carry heavy rag bags several blocks back and forth all day long. The load overburdened their still-developing bone structures. The calisthenics and dance exercises were also good for children who, in the absence of good lighting, sat hunched over worktables for hours at a time. While she may not have thought of it as physical therapy, she understood the importance of providing positive stress to other parts of the body to counterbalance the stresses imposed by physical labor.

By this time Eleanor had begun dating Franklin, who was then a senior at Harvard. Although she had known him since childhood, her time at Allenswood and his time at Groton and Harvard had meant they had not seen each other for a number of years. She enthusiastically told him about her work and invited him to visit the settlement. Although the Reverend Endicott Peabody had required his students to do social work as part of their education, what Franklin had seen in the environs of Groton, Massachusetts, had not prepared him for what he would see in New York's tenement houses.

The Rivington Street Settlement House where Eleanor began her work among the poor. The Survey, 1914.

Two-thirds of the city in 1903 lived in some ninety thousand tenement apartments on the Lower East Side. Most of them were unspeakably gloomy. Ten of the fourteen rooms on each floor had no windows.[6] Although New York State had passed a law in 1901 requiring landlords to install indoor toilets in all new construction, the tenements Eleanor visited had backyard privies that emptied directly into the city's overburdened sewers. Typhus, cholera, and tuberculosis ran rampant under these conditions.

Labor historian Brigid O'Farrell describes an episode where a little girl had taken ill. Eleanor took Franklin to visit the tenement where the child lived. "When we got out on the street afterward," Eleanor wrote, "he drew a long breath of air. Not fresh air, there in those crowded, smelly streets with pushcarts at the curb. But better than the air in that tenement. 'My God,' he said, aghast, 'I didn't know people lived like that!'" O'Farrell notes that Eleanor and her "feller," as the children called Franklin, "began an education that profoundly affected their views of the world."[7]

There were far too many people who did not know people lived like that, and Eleanor believed that nothing would change until people had the facts. Her life in a sacramental tradition may have been the source of a subliminal recognition that people must see in order to believe. From her Junior League work, she would be drawn to the fact-finding mission of the National Consumers League.

The League was created to urge people to use their power as consumers to advance workplace safety and to address working conditions and child labor. "Members of the League evaluated retail stores and urged women to patronize only those stores . . . which had been found to follow policies of equal pay for equal work, a ten-hour workday, and a minimum wage of $6 per week."[8]

As with her trips to Rivington Street, Eleanor was not without fear as she undertook fact-finding missions for the League. "In those days, these people often worked at home, and I felt I had no right to invade their private dwellings, to ask questions, to investigate conditions. I was frightened to death. But this was what had been required of me and I wanted to be useful. I entered my first sweatshop and walked up the steps of my first tenement. . . . I saw little children of four and five sitting at tables until they dropped with fatigue and earning tragically little a week. Conditions of employment were such that the workers were often in real physical danger."[9] From Henry Satterlee's Sunday school curriculum to William Grosvenor's preaching, her church's emphasis on duty was so fully internalized that she knew she had to do what she was asked even though she was "frightened to death." Duty taking precedence over fear would be a recurring theme throughout Eleanor's life. It was also something she shared with the man she would marry.

In writing to Franklin in the fall of 1903, she commented enthusiastically on a poem he had written and included in his previous letter. She especially liked the line "fear nothing and be faithful unto death."[10]

Late in life she summarized her understanding of fear and courage. "Courage is more exhilarating than fear and in the long run it is easier. We do not have to become heroes overnight. Just a step at time, meeting each thing that comes up, seeing it is not as dreadful as it appeared, discovering we have the strength to stare it down."[11] But this way of understanding fear did not mean she was fear*less*. There would be many more things to fear along the way.

FRANKLIN ASKS HER TO MARRY HIM

On Sunday, November 22, 1903, Franklin joined Eleanor for church in the morning (and chapel that evening). At the end of the day, he asked her to marry him.

Sara Delano Roosevelt was concerned to learn that Franklin had proposed. Although she had known Eleanor since her birth, she had hoped her son would not consider marriage until after he had completed law school. She thought Franklin at twenty-one and Eleanor at nineteen were both too young. Grandmother Hall was less resistant, and so a compromise was worked out. The couple's engagement would be kept secret for at least one year and would be public for another year.

On St. Patrick's Day 1905, the fifth cousins once removed were married in the home of Eleanor's godmother (and second cousin) Susie Parish with FDR's mentor from Groton, the Reverend Endicott Peabody, officiating. The date was chosen because Eleanor's godfather would be expected to give her away, but Uncle Teddy was now president of the United States. March 17 was a convenient date because the president would need to be in town for the St. Patrick's Day parade.

Marie Souvestre sent a telegram expressing love and good wishes.

The couple embarked on a European honeymoon. Eleanor had planned to visit Souvestre and introduce her to Franklin when they arrived in England. Unfortunately, Marie had died just two weeks after their wedding day. Eleanor did, nonetheless, visit Allenswood, but she said it was just not the same without her mentor.

When the young couple returned to New York, they moved into Sara Roosevelt's double town house on East Sixty-Fifth Street (now the Roosevelt House Public Policy Institute, owned by Hunter College). They also spent as much time as possible at Springwood, the Roosevelt estate in Hyde Park.

Springwood was a good fit for Eleanor. It was about twenty miles south of her grandmother's estate in Tivoli. Both estates were on high ground overlooking the Hudson River, but it was still possible to hear the gentle click-clack of the train running at river-level below. Whether southbound to New York City or northbound to Albany and Montreal, to this day the trains sound a gentle whistle as they pass Hyde Park. Eleanor would grow to love Springwood and the Roosevelt parish church, St. James', Hyde Park.

The Roosevelt family had a long history with St. James' Episcopal Church. FDR's father and his older half brother

James were vestrymen. FDR himself would begin serving in 1906 and continue even during his years in the White House.

As part of its social mission, St. James' sponsored a free circulating library that would be the town's only library until 1927, when a public library opened. Sara Roosevelt was the principal patron of the St. James' library.[12]

When she began writing her "My Day" columns in the 1930s, St. James' Church was often mentioned. Sometimes the references were indirect, e.g., "After church, we . . ." Other times it might refer to the rector bringing his children over for a swim. If the column was about something in Hyde Park, the church in question was always St. James'. On one occasion it was about Ascension, the little church next to Holy Cross Monastery across the river. Eleanor opened a flower show there in 1946. Why? It had been founded by St. James one hundred years earlier.[13]

About six months after their wedding, FDR continued his legal studies, and Eleanor found she would have another opportunity to "stare down" her fear. She found that she was pregnant. A friend who was also expecting her first child at that time told her, "I'm really not afraid of having a baby. Everyone has to be born. If so many people can go through it successfully, why shouldn't I?" Eleanor said she had not been expressing her own fears in words because she felt it would have shocked her husband and mother-in-law, but she was frightened until she realized the baby would come when it was ready regardless of what she herself might be feeling. "I found myself gradually acquiring the discipline I needed for the final ordeal. I never again was afraid of bearing a child."[14] It was a good thing she had stared down the fear. There would be five more pregnancies. Anna, her first child, was born in May 1906. James followed in December 1907. Franklin Jr. was born in March 1909 but died three months later. Despite her grief, she became pregnant again. In September 1910, Elliott was born. A second Franklin Jr. was born in September 1914, and finally John in March 1916.

With so many babies so close in succession, it is not surprising that Eleanor stepped back from her activism.

"I had lost a good deal of my crusading spirit where the poor were concerned, because I had been told that I had no right to go into the slums or into the hospitals, for fear of bringing diseases home to my children, so I had fallen into the easier way of sitting on boards and giving small sums to this or that charity and thinking the whole of my duty to my neighbor was done."[15]

The year Elliott was born, FDR was elected to the New York State Senate. The family took a house in Albany and began worshipping at the Cathedral of All Saints, where her friend Alice Morgan Wright was a member. Wright was a sculptor who would exhibit at the controversial New York Armory Show in 1913, which introduced modern art to the United States. She is acknowledged as a major influence on the development of cubism in the United States.[16]

Wright was also an advocate of women's suffrage. Eleanor was not: "I had never given the question serious thought, for I took it for granted that men were superior creatures and knew more about politics than women did, and while I realized that if my husband was a suffragist, I probably must be, too, I cannot claim to have been a feminist in those early days."[17]

Needless to say, she changed her mind. When Wright became a founding member of the League of Women Voters, Eleanor served as vice president of legislative affairs.[18]

Eleanor enjoyed life in Albany, noting that the house where they lived was the first home in which she was in charge. Both Springwood and Sixty-Fifth Street were Sara's domains, as well as Campobello, their summer residence in Canada. The Albany house was Eleanor's. However, they would not be there for long. In 1913, President Woodrow Wilson named FDR assistant secretary of the Navy.

THE MOVE TO WASHINGTON

Eleanor's Auntie Bye, who was married to Rear Admiral William Sheffield Cowles, had a house in Washington's Dupont Circle neighborhood, which Eleanor had visited many times. It was known as the "Little White House" because Bye's brother Teddy often sought refuge there during his presidency. Franklin and Eleanor took up residence at Auntie Bye's house, and Eleanor gave birth to her last two sons before the family would return to New York in 1920.

At the time of the Roosevelt's arrival, Dupont Circle was home to an assortment of young progressives of both major parties (and a few minor ones) often living in shared quarters in what had become a newly fashionable neighborhood near Georgetown. They included future notables, such as Walter Lippmann, one of the founding editors of *The New Republic*; Felix Frankfurter, whom FDR would one day appoint to the Supreme Court; John Foster Dulles, who would later work with Eleanor at the United Nations; and Sumner Welles, who had served as a page at the Roosevelts' wedding and would become undersecretary of state in the New Deal.[19]

If Eleanor had any thoughts of continuing the retreat from public life she began with the birth of her first child, she was soon disabused of that notion. As the wife of an assistant cabinet secretary, she found herself facing a demanding array of official duties and quasi-official expectations. She proved equal to the task, but the demands on her time were so great that she hired a social secretary to manage her crowded appointments calendar. Hospital visitations were regular obligations, especially after World War I began, when her duties were expanded to include working in a Red Cross canteen and supervising a knitting room in the Navy Department to make sweaters and scarves for the sailors.

Eleanor took special interest in her husband's growing involvement with trade unions, which she attributed to Louis Howe, a former Albany newspaperman who accompanied him to Washington as his secretary. "Howe insisted that FDR find out about labor conditions in the navy yards, which were his special province in the department. . . . With Howe at his side, Roosevelt invited the unions in and asked them to teach him."[20]

This involvement would be significant to both Roosevelts in their later work. It was during these busy years in Washington that we see an early example of what would come to be Eleanor's trademark *modus operandi*. Whenever there was a need to build bridges, Eleanor would arrange a luncheon, a tea, a picnic, or a scrambled eggs supper—a meaningful meal intended to build relationships, rather like the Eucharist itself.

In this instance, Eleanor had learned from friends at the British embassy who were responsible for reporting on labor matters that they were having difficulty getting information. They had to rely on newspapers, which meant they had no opportunity to ask questions or see things for themselves. Eleanor was well-aware that the American Federation of Labor had a building in Washington full of people who would be eager to talk, and she mentioned that to one of the embassy friends. But she also realized that as a diplomat (and an Englishman!), it would be awkward if not impossible for him to call on people he did not know. Enter the "hospitality solution." Eleanor arranged for a luncheon with several heads of various unions. From that time on, she said, the British "were able to write more comprehensive reports, as they could verify newspaper stories by actual contact with the people involved."[21]

How, we might ask, did Eleanor happen to have friends at the British embassy? The Roosevelts were not in the diplomatic corps, but they *were* members of St. Thomas' Church, Dupont Circle. There is a high probability that some British diplomats were too.

The Roosevelt's remained close to the church during their Washington years. FDR was elected to the vestry of St. Thomas' Church in 1918. During the family's summer visits to Campobello, they worshiped at St. Anne's Anglican Church and invited parishioners to bring their friends and neighbors to picnics at the Roosevelt cottage.

Following World War I, a deadly flu pandemic, sometimes called the "Spanish Flu," spread throughout the world. For Eleanor, it meant additional responsibilities:

> Every member of my family came down with flu, my husband and all five children. I was able to get a nurse for Elliott, who also had pneumonia. The other five I nursed myself. This was one of the occasions when I was grateful for my grandmother's stern training. I had kept myself in good condition and I was able to cope with nursing five members of my own family and to make my rounds with the soup [distributed by cabinet wives and others to temporary shelters around Washington], talking to the sick girls in the shelter. With a house filled with flu patients, I had no reason to fear infection from the outside.[22]

During and after the war, she also continued her hospital visits to wounded soldiers, an activity that required her to "stare down" her fear once again. The Red Cross had asked her to visit St. Elizabeth's Hospital, where the Navy had a facility for men who had gone temporarily or permanently insane.

"I cannot do this, I thought. I was terrified of insanity. Then I realized that I was the Assistant Secretary's wife. This was my job. I had to do it whether I could do it or not." When she entered the ward, the doctor locked the door behind them. "Locked in with the insane! I wanted to bang at the door, to get out. But I was ashamed of myself. I would not have shown my terror for the world." She described a scene in which men were in cubicles, often chained to their beds. All seemed to be mumbling and talking to themselves.[23]

> [At the end of the room] stood a young boy with fair hair. The sun in the window placed high up, well above the patients' heads, touched his hair and seemed almost like a halo. He was talking to himself incessantly, and I inquired what he was saying. "He is giving the orders," said the doctor, "which were given every night at Dunkirk, where he was stationed." I remembered my husband's telling me that he had been in Dunkirk and that every evening the enemy planes came over the town and bombed it and the entire population was ordered down into the cellars. This boy had stood the strain of the nightly bombing until he could stand it no longer, then he went insane.[24]

The toll was physical, emotional, and philosophical. "There was, of course, a certain amount of pure physical fatigue from walking miles of hospital wards day after day, but that was nothing in comparison with the horrible consciousness of waste and feeling of resentment that burned within me as I wondered why men could not sit down around a table and settle their difference before an infinite number of youth of many nations had to suffer." She said the "horror at seeing people who had broken mentally and emotionally made me lie awake nights."[25]

In addition to the labor and housing concerns that continued to attract her interest, the elimination of war was gaining a place on her agenda, something that began to surface even before the United States entered World War I.

When William Jennings Bryan was secretary of state, Eleanor said anti-war sentiments "must have been stirring in me even then." Bryan had "miniature plowshares made from old guns and given to many people in the government. These were greeted by some with ridicule, but to me they were not in the least ridiculous. I thought them an excellent reminder that our swords should be made into plowshares and should continue in this useful occupation."[26]

Over time, the prayer attributed to Saint Francis of Assisi, "Lord, make me an instrument of your peace . . ." would become a favorite. She had two copies: one to be carried in her purse and another framed and placed in her bedroom.

Racial concerns also became more acute in 1919, when Attorney General A. Mitchell Palmer began a series of raids in response to the "Red Scare" following the war. The Justice Department was infiltrating labor unions and rounding up and deporting anyone thought to be communist, anarchist, or socialist. In an act of defiance, a bomb was exploded outside Palmer's residence in the same neighborhood where the Roosevelts were living. In the midst of this strife, race riots also erupted. Eleanor wrote to a friend that ideas, habits, and customs had to be "revolutionized" lest the country experience another type of revolution. Eleanor began by replacing her all-white household staff with black workers. For the rest of her life, she would be an advocate for racial justice.[27]

The family's return to New York the next year was anything but quiet. The Democratic National Convention had nominated Franklin to be the vice presidential running mate of Ohio governor and fellow Episcopalian James N. Cox. The 1920 race against Warren G. Harding and his running mate Calvin Coolidge was Eleanor's first experience on the campaign trail. It would not be her last. Over the course of the campaign, FDR made eight hundred speeches in support of joining the League of Nations, a cause also dear to Eleanor's heart. She believed it was the only way that could prevent war. Her work with the United Nations late in life would fulfill many of the hopes both Roosevelts had for the League.

DEFEAT, TRAGEDY, AND TRANSFORMATION

The Harding-Coolidge ticket won in a landslide, but neither Franklin nor Eleanor seemed especially disheartened. Franklin began thinking in terms of running for governor of New York. In the summer of 1921, the family departed for Campobello. Franklin was hoping to stay for an extended period, and his trusted advisor Louis Howe would join them to help plan the gubernatorial campaign. Then tragedy struck. Franklin was stricken with poliomyelitis. Eleanor effectively became a full-time nurse for the next year. She described the following winter as the most difficult of her life. Fortunately, Franklin maintained a positive outlook throughout, and as it became clear that, with assistance, he would be able to resume his professional life, Eleanor invested her energy in keeping Franklin interested in politics and civic affairs.

Eleanor began volunteering with the newly formed Women's Division of the New York State Democratic Party, and Franklin accepted appointments to the board of trustees of the Cathedral of St. John the Divine and St. Stephen's (now Bard) College. In 1923, he was appointed to the diocesan Social Services Commission. That same year, Eleanor joined the Women's Trade Union League and the Women's City Club. Both groups through Eleanor would become a valued source of information and political connection for Franklin.

Eleanor had her first contact with the Women's Trade Union League before she and Franklin left Washington. The League had been created in 1903 by women trade unionists and social reformers, such as Vida Scudder and Jane Addams. Its membership consisted of women who were union members and anyone, including men, in sympathy with the aims and aspirations of the labor movement. The stated objectives of the organization were aiding women workers to organize and assisting those already organized to work for improved working conditions. These improvements could include starting clubs and lunchrooms for women working in factories and helping arrange entertainment for workers.[28]

Eleanor met Rose Schneiderman, one of the group's chief organizers, in 1922 when the organization could boast twenty years of activism. Schneiderman had come to public attention in 1911 with her blistering critique of the "good people of New York" at the mass meeting following the infamous Triangle Factory Fire. Now facing a huge backlash against unions in the aftermath of World War I, Schneiderman was concerned that factionalism within the organization was distracting from work that needed to be done. She had the idea of buying a house where the women could meet for classes and parties, with costs offset by a cafeteria. For help in raising money among society women, she turned to Dorothy Straight.

Dorothy Payne Whitney Straight was a member of Grace Church on Broadway, which once housed the New York Training School for Deaconesses. She had absorbed the teachings of William Reed Huntington and his successors as well as the parish's social service ethos. At the age of fifteen, she inherited a large fortune from her parents and dedicated her life to social and economic justice. With her husband, Willard Straight, she cofounded *The New Republic*, the progressive journal of public affairs, and The New School for Social Research. She was a veteran of the Junior League, which by 1921 had grown to be a national organization. That same year, she was elected the first president of the national federation. A few years younger than Eleanor, the two had been friends for a number of years.

Dorothy agreed to chair a committee to raise funds for the clubhouse Rose Schneiderman envisioned. The campaign began at her house with a tea for her friends, Eleanor included. It was Eleanor's first meeting with the legendary firebrand. Eleanor told Rose she thought the clubhouse was a very good idea and assured her of her support, thus beginning a collaboration that would continue for the next forty years.

Following the tea, Eleanor invited Rose to the Roosevelt town house on Sixty-Fifth Street for one of what eventually became her famous scrambled eggs suppers. By her own admission, Eleanor had never really learned to cook, but she knew how to scramble eggs. She would place a chafing dish on the dining room table and scramble eggs while she talked with her guests, who enjoyed the informality.

The social gatherings were soon expanded to Hyde Park and Campobello, giving FDR the opportunity to get to know Schneiderman and her associates. Rose recalled the Val-Kill Brook by Eleanor's cottage in which she said she "once had the temerity to take FDR rowing." Sara Roosevelt usually joined in the fun too. Eleanor's daughter Anna, now seventeen, also joined the league.

Upon joining the league, Eleanor focused her attention on the finance committee, arranging luncheons and introducing Schneiderman to Astors and Vanderbilts and other potential patrons. The family hosted a Christmas party for the children of unemployed workers, "complete with a decorated Christmas tree, a magic show and singing, and ice cream and cake for each child. The two youngest boys, Franklin Jr. and Johnny, became 'deputies for Santa Claus,' and FDR joined in the festivities the first year by reading aloud from the classic *A Christmas Carol*."[29]

Eleanor also poured herself into the league's educational activities, helping to find volunteer instructors from Columbia University's Teachers College and recruiting students for the Bryn Mawr Summer School for Women in Industry.

In addition to WTUL and the League of Women Votes, Eleanor jointed the Women's International League for Peace and Freedom and the Women's City Club. The club had been created in 1915 specifically because women were not permitted to join the august good government group, the City Club of New York. Frances Perkins had joined with a number of other reform-minded women to organize an alternative that would have significant success in its advocacy of social service and social justice. It continues to exist today under the name Women Creating Change. Perkins outlined the club's program for civic education. The club became a tireless advocate for the abolition of child labor, and it succeeded in obtaining a ban on sex discrimination in New York State's civil service. It won admission of women to Columbia Law School and sponsored the Maternity Center Association at a time when New York City was one of the most dangerous places in the world to give birth. Their activities were credited with improving infant survival by

29 percent and reducing maternal deaths by 60 percent citywide.[30]

Although the club was not a church-based organization, there was no shortage of prominent Episcopal church women among the activists. In addition to Frances Perkins, there was Frances' and Eleanor's mutual friend the intrepid Mary Harriman along with Virginia Gildersleeve, dean of Barnard College; Cornelia Bryce Pinchot, wife of the celebrated conservation governor of Pennsylvania, Gifford Pinchot; writer-activist Mary van Kleeck, of the Russell Sage Foundation; Pauline Morton Sabin, president of the Women's National Republican Club; Helen Rogers Reid, of the *New York Herald Tribune*; and Mary Simkhovitch, founder of Greenwich House. In 1923, Eleanor Roosevelt would join their ranks. She would chair the club's city planning unit and subsequently serve as first vice president.

The credibility of Franklin and Eleanor Roosevelt as friends of labor in the mid-1920s showed that lay leaders of the diocese were capable of expanding ties with the labor movement that the late Bishop Potter had forged in the years before Franklin and Eleanor were born. In 1925 when Bishop William Thomas Manning asked FDR to chair the capital campaign for the cathedral, the legacy of that alliance began to take tangible form. The week before FDR would keynote the kickoff event at Madison Square Garden, the bishop announced that the Central Trades and Labor Council and the Building Trades Council had formed a committee to seek contributions from five-hundred-member unions. Gordon G. Young of the Granite Cutters

International Association spoke at the kickoff event, along with the Catholic mayor of New York, John F. Hylan.

The dignity of labor was ultimately incorporated into the cathedral's architecture. St. Benedict's quote "to work is to pray" is carved into the wall of the Labor Bay. Above the quote are stained-glass windows depicting printers, construction engineers, blacksmiths, and numerous other trades. The seven chapels behind the high altar are each named for a patron saint from the homelands of the immigrant groups who built New York.

RETURN TO ALBANY

In 1928, Eleanor energetically served in Governor Al Smith's campaign for the presidency, while FDR campaigned for the governorship. By now a veteran campaigner, she was nonetheless appalled by the anti-Catholic prejudice she encountered. She said "the kind of propaganda that some of the religious groups, aided and abetted by the opposition, put forth in that campaign utterly disgusted me. If I needed anything to show me what prejudice can do to the intelligence of human beings, that campaign was the best lesson I have had."[31]

Al Smith lost his bid for the presidency, but FDR was elected governor. The Roosevelts returned to Albany and the Cathedral of All Saints, this time taking up residence in the governor's mansion. Despite having a panoply of official duties as the first lady of New York, Eleanor was determined to chart her own course. She spent four days a week in Albany and then three days in New York teaching at the Todhunter School for Girls, now a part of the Dalton School. In time, Eleanor became vice principal of the school, but her activism did not subside.

For the twenty-fifth anniversary of the WTUL, Eleanor once again turned to the "hospitality solution," this time on a grand scale. Saturday, June 8, 1929, began early in the morning with league members in New York City boarding a boat for Poughkeepsie, where buses would take them to Springwood. Prominent New Yorkers joined the factory women on the ride. Rose Schneiderman recalled a beautiful sunny day "and a warm breeze that rippled the water in the harbor would also stir the stifling hot air in the sweatshops and the laundries, the tenements and crowded streets of Manhattan's Lower East Side, all left behind for the day."[32]

Eleanor reminded the newly minted governor that he would have the starring role, although the women would also present a pageant at 3 p.m. "Pantomime and songs told the story of working girls: the shirtwaist strikes of 1909, the devastating Triangle Company fire, employer resistance, and police brutality. . . . They educated as they sang and danced" before an audience of four hundred guests gathered on the rolling lawns overlooking the Hudson.

Governor Roosevelt announced the creation of a commission to make recommendations for an old-age pension law for the state, long a goal of the league. He went on to state his belief that the workers who contribute to the wealth and prosperity of the commonwealth are entitled to enjoy its benefits.

If Father Huntington, the aging founder of the Church Association for the Advancement of the Interests of Labor, was watching from the cloister of his monastery across the river, no doubt he would have been pleased.

CHAPTER FIVE

KEEPING AT TASKS TOO HARD FOR US

By the time Eleanor adopted her nightly prayer, she was already adept at navigating the implications of its petition: "Keep us at tasks too hard for us that we may be driven to thee for strength." It had been an overarching theme of her life.

Faced with the possibility that her husband's promising career as a public servant might be permanently derailed by the effects of polio, she succeeded in keeping both his interest in politics and his political profile high. In 1928, he had been elected governor of what was then the largest and richest state in the union. Then, just five months after the WTUL celebrated its anniversary in the joyous and hope-filled gathering at Hyde Park, the stock market crashed. Wall Street millionaires jumped out windows, bread lines formed, and "Hoovervilles" sprung up across the country as the suddenly unemployed lost their homes. None of the protections we take for granted today were in place. By 1932, one out of every four people in the workforce were unemployed. In Toledo and other industrial centers, the figure was as high as 80 percent.

Eleanor knew that Franklin wanted to be president, even amidst the worst depression the world had ever known. She did everything she could to support that goal even though she feared that life in the White House would be a kind of gilded captivity for her. While the Democratic National Convention deliberated in Chicago, the Roosevelts and their inner circle gathered in the study of the Governor's Mansion in Albany. As word arrived that FDR had scored the nomination, a kind of pandemonium broke out. Eleanor hugged FDR's secretary, Missy LeHand. Two of her sons shook hands as though they were meeting for the first time. Papers flew in the air. Everybody congratulated everybody. And then Eleanor soberly announced that she was going to go scramble some eggs![1]

For the next four months, the popular song "Happy Days Are Here Again" would play incessantly throughout the country as the campaign rolled on to a landslide victory for FDR. But when inauguration day rolled around, Eleanor was anything but happy.

The day before the inauguration, she managed to exit undetected from Washington's Mayflower Hotel by slipping out the rear entrance at 7:15 in the morning. A cab awaited with friend and soulmate, Lorena Hickok, in the back seat. "Hick," as she was affectionately known, was an Associated

Press reporter assigned to cover Eleanor, who had become a close friend. It was Hickok who would encourage Eleanor to begin writing her "My Day" column. By the time of the inauguration, the relationship had deepened significantly. Hick eventually lived in the White House along with other close advisors, such as Louis Howe and Harry Hopkins, and some of the Roosevelt grandchildren. In this historic moment before the inauguration, Eleanor needed a trusted confidante by her side, and Hick was more than willing to oblige.[2]

Eleanor asked the driver to take them to the Rock Creek Cemetery. Created in 1719 from the glebe lands granted to St. Paul's Church in the Rock Creek parish, the vestry had expanded it in 1791 to serve the whole city as both a burial ground and a public park.

Eleanor directed the driver to a grove of trees and asked him to park there and wait for them. The two women walked across the wet grass and sat on the semicircular bench in front of a sculpture Hickok had heard of but never actually seen. It was by Augustus Saint-Gaudens, the elder brother of the sculptor whose work adorned the Church of the Incarnation, where young Eleanor worshipped as she worked through her grief at the loss of her parents and younger brother. It is doubtful that Eleanor knew that Saint-Gaudens had been drawn into the Episcopal Church through his relationship with Phillips Brooks, the brother of her first rector at Incarnation. What is clear is that his work, like his brother's, continued to have the ability to move her.

The formal name of the sculpture in the cemetery is *The Mystery of the Hereafter and The Peace of God that Passeth Understanding*. Colloquially, it is known simply as *Grief*.

Also known as the Adams Memorial, the sculpture is a bronze figure of a woman seated against a granite block, hooded and draped in cloth, with her eyes cast downward and her right hand touching her chin. The author and historian Henry Adams had commissioned the work as a memorial to his wife.

Eleanor derived solace and strength from frequent visits to Augustus Saint-Gaudens's portrait of grief in the park created by St. Paul's Church, Rock Creek, in Washington, D.C. Saint-Gaudens was the elder brother of the sculptor whose work adorned Eleanor's parish church in New York. Courtesy of the National Parks Service.

After a long silence, Eleanor told her friend that when the Roosevelts first lived in Washington, she was "much younger and not very wise." Whenever she was feeling unhappy and sorry for herself, she would make her way out to the memorial "and sit and look at that woman." She said she would always come away somehow feeling better and stronger. Then she abruptly "blurted out" that she could not go through with the inauguration. She could *not* be first lady.[3] It was the same feeling that had overwhelmed her years earlier when she was expected to visit the soldiers who had gone insane. She now feared being a "state prisoner" as Martha Washington once described herself.[4] She believed she could not do it, but it turned out that she could.

Although she would not encounter her nightly prayer for another seven years, it is not difficult to imagine that she prayed for strength in the face of something that seemed too hard. Like Jesus in the Garden of Gethsemane agonizing over his fate, Eleanor acknowledged and articulated her grief about what was to come, then, like Jesus, quietly accepted her fate, as if a cathartic moment had been followed by a kind of peace.

NOTHING TO FEAR BUT FEAR ITSELF

That night, because the nation's circumstances were so dire, with banks failing right and left, the members of FDR's cabinet were sworn in so they could begin work immediately. Frances Perkins recalled that they all listened intently as the president presented the draft of his inaugural address.

The line that went down in history—"the only thing we have to fear is fear itself"—was not in the draft they had heard. Perkins said it was added late in the night after they had all left. Forever thereafter when someone commented on it, Roosevelt would go silent and look downward, as if bowing his head. She was convinced that he believed God had given him that language.[5]

"Fear nothing and be faithful unto death," he had written in his poem for Eleanor during their courtship. It seemed to have stayed with the president and with Eleanor too. Late in life she talked about what she had learned about fear. "You gain strength, courage, and confidence by every experience in which you really stop to look fear in the face. You are able to say to yourself, 'I lived through this horror. I can take the next thing that comes along.' The danger lies in refusing to face the fear, in not daring to come to grips with it. If you fail anywhere along the line, it will take away your confidence. You must make yourself succeed every time. *You must do the thing you think you cannot do.*"[6]

She thought she could not be First Lady, but she came to be widely regarded as the greatest First Lady of all time. Her habit of asking God for strength when faced with something "too hard" enabled her to "stare down" the fear. A poem Louis Howe composed for her reminded her of what she already believed. The poem referred to her fears as a ghostlike brotherhood that would vanish as soon as she stared it in the face.[7] Both staring at the bronze interpretation of grief and saying out loud that she could not do what was expected of her was the moment in which she came face-to-face with this example of fear barring the pleasant path. Soon she was able to settle into the comfortable sentiment of an inspirational work she already carried in her purse, along with the Prayer of St. Francis. It was a meditation by poet, Princeton professor, and Presbyterian clergyman Henry van Dyke Jr., entitled *The Foot-Path to Peace*:

> To be glad of life, because it gives you the chance to love and to work and to play and to look up at the stars. To be satisfied with your possessions, but not contended with yourself until you have made the best of them. To despise nothing in the world except falsehood and meanness, and to fear nothing except cowardice. To be governed by your admirations rather than by your disgusts; to covet nothing that is your neighbor's except his kindness of heart and gentleness of manners. To think seldom of your enemies, often of your friends, and every day of Christ; and to spend as much time as you can, with body and with spirit, in God's out-of-doors. These are little guide-posts on the foot-path to peace.[8]

Eleanor circled "Christ" and added "with yourself" after the word "peace."[9]

THE COSTS AND BENEFITS OF BEING FIRST LADY

It was not long before Eleanor began to see that there would be rewards as well as sacrifices in her role as First

Lady. It gave her, as van Dyke's poem suggested, another "chance to love"—this time with even greater reach than before. Because of her national visibility, she immediately began receiving letters in the White House for causes that sometimes attracted not just her sympathy but sometimes her personal wealth. An early example was a letter from a Brooklyn man whose fourteen-year-old sister had scoliosis of the spine and needed an operation that the family could not afford.

Eleanor was moved to action by an awareness of the toll the disease had taken on her Auntie Bye in recent years as well as her own memory of wearing a brace as a child. Eleanor forwarded the letter to the head of New York's Orthopedic Hospital, which her Grandfather Roosevelt had helped to found. She asked if a bed could be made available at no charge. The answer was affirmative. The operation proceeded. Eleanor made her way to New York to visit the girl, who would remain in the hospital for the next ten months. Despite the long recuperation, she was said to be in good spirits, no doubt thanks to additional visits from the First Lady, supplemented with flowers, fruit, candy, books, and holiday gifts. Eleanor stayed in touch with the family, eventually finding jobs for both the girl and her brother. Years later, Eleanor attended the wedding of the healthy young woman she had helped. When a little one came along, Eleanor stood as godmother.[10]

Not all of her passions had such happy outcomes. During her first year in the White House there were thirty-three lynchings—African Americans murdered by white mobs.

They were among an astounding total of some 3,500 such murders in the course of Eleanor's lifetime. Although most lynchings occurred in the Deep South, in 1933 three thousand men, women, and children had overwhelmed fifty Maryland state troopers to kill a man on the Eastern Shore of the Chesapeake, just 138 miles from the White House.

FDR condemned the killing in a radio address and in a speech before the Federal Council of Churches. "This new generation," he said, "is not content with preachings against that vile form of collective murder—lynch law—which has broken out in our midst anew. We know that it is murder, and a deliberate and definite disobedience of the Commandment, 'Thou shalt not kill.' We do not excuse those in high places or in low who condone lynch law."[11]

Despite the strength of the condemnation, he stopped short of endorsing a bill that would have made lynching a federal crime. Eleanor, along with many others, believed that a federal law was necessary because state and local officials frequently declined to prosecute lynchings. Part of the reason was that they undoubtedly feared the strength of the mobs, but another more chilling reason was that they were sometimes a part of the lynching itself.

Eleanor pressed her husband to the extent that she could. His refusal to endorse the bill was based on his certainty that Southern Democrats would retaliate against all the other New Deal programs. Doubting that she would ever persuade him, she took another tack. In 1934, she joined the NAACP and maintained a steady correspondence with Walter White, the executive director. No doubt she viewed with approval his correspondence about a mass meeting against lynching planned for the Broadway Tabernacle, a Congregational church on Manhattan's Upper West Side. The impressive list of endorsers included both of her New York bishops, William Thomas Manning and Charles K. Gilbert, and a former rector, Howard Chandler Robbins, as well as her labor movement colleague, Lucy Randolph Mason, the daughter and granddaughter of Episcopal priests from Virginia. It also included the rector of Grace Church, Walter Russell Bowie, who had edited *The Harvard Crimson* with FDR. Religious leaders from other traditions were well-represented, too, along with celebrated writers such as Pearl Buck, a one-time Presbyterian missionary, and Dorothy Day, founder of the Catholic Worker Movement.

For the rest of her life, Eleanor would promote federal antilynching legislation in every way she could—through speeches, published writings, and, no doubt, prayer. In 2022, sixty years after her death, it finally became law.

Through the ensuing decades she faced constant criticism, including death threats. By 1950, the Ku Klux Klan had become so exasperated by her relentless, high-profile advocacy that it put a bounty on her head of twenty-five thousand dollars, an amount which would be worth more than three hundred thousand dollars in today's currency. The notion that she was dangerous was not confined to vigilante groups. She had been on J. Edgar Hoover's watch list for twenty-six years.

During the 1920s, intense infighting between liberals, socialists, and communists had damaged the International

Ladies' Garment Workers Union. "Red-baiting"—accusing people of being communists or communist sympathizers as a means of discrediting them or their political arguments—ran rampant. Rose Schneiderman and a number of Eleanor's associates from the WTUL were members of the union. Eleanor became a vocal critic of red-baiting both within the labor movement and from the outside, a stand that engendered direct attacks on her as a "fellow traveler." The problem began in 1924 when Eleanor was selected to be a judge in the Bok Peace Prize essay competition. Biographer Balance Wiesen Cook said it was Eleanor's first experience of the "kind of public criticism that would remain a feature of her life."[12]

Created by Pulitzer Prize–winning author Edward William Bok, the Dutch-born editor of the *Ladies' Home Journal*, the prize offered one hundred thousand dollars to the person submitting the best practical plan for the United States to cooperate with other nations to promote world peace. In his writings, Bok had noted that although the United States might have gone to war to "make the world safe for democracy," in Woodrow Wilson's words, five years after the armistice, the government had done nothing to advance the cause of world peace, refusing even to join Wilson's brainchild, the League of Nations.[13]

FDR, despite his vigorous support for the League in his 1920 vice presidential campaign, had lost faith in it. He entered the essay competition with a plan encouraging the creation of a new international organization to replace the League; however, he withdrew it when Eleanor was named a judge. She had been recruited by Esther Lape, a League of Women Voters colleague, who had agreed to administer the competition.

The winning essay, from Charles Herbert Levermore, former president of Adelphi College, proposed US adherence to the Permanent Court of International Justice and the extension of cooperation with the League of Nations. It did not actually call for the United States to join the League.

The plan, which was presented to the Senate as part of the competition's design, was widely criticized as propaganda for the League of Nations. "Senate isolationists were outraged and called for an investigation into the un-American and potentially treasonous nature of the Bok Award."[14] When it was learned that the committee of judges were all women, the criticism intensified. Eleanor's FBI file was opened that same year and continued to grow through the ensuing decades.

STRENGTH FOR THE HARSH CRITICISM

It was not just the hard tasks Eleanor undertook that required strength. Her ability to weather the criticism and threats with grace and a determination to continue required strength too. No doubt much of her strength stemmed from her deep confidence in the rightness of her various causes—causes which, when fully understood, can be seen as outgrowths of her basic intention to love her neighbor. It was an intention that received continual reinforcement through her life in the church. In addition to the preaching and the mission activities of her parishes, there was the ongoing subliminal effect of liturgical prayer and hymnody. Both the moral thrust of preaching and the lessons learned from widespread mission activity among the poor and disadvantaged had so fully permeated the Episcopal Church by the dawn of the twentieth century that the 1928 revision of the Book of Common Prayer included a prayer for social justice: “Almighty God, who has created man in thine own image; Grant us grace fearlessly to contend against evil, and to make no peace with oppression; and, that we may reverently use our freedom, help us to employ it in the maintenance of justice among men and nations, to the glory of thy holy Name; through Jesus Christ our Lord, who lives and reigns with you and the Holy Spirit, one God, now and for ever. *Amen*.”[15]

Two other prayers imply a desire for racial and ethnic harmony. “For the Unity of God’s People” asked God to “take away all hatred and prejudice, and whatsoever else may hinder us from godly union and concord.”[16] A prayer “For Our Country” included a petition to “defend our liberties, and fashion into one united people the multitudes brought hither out of many kindred tongues.”

A prayer for Christian service sought a blessing on all who “give themselves to the service of their fellow men” and that they may worthily minister to “the suffering, the friendless, and the needy.” The prayer “For Every Man in his Work” pleaded, “Deliver us, we beseech thee, in our several callings, from the service of mammon, that we may do the work which thou givest us to do, in truth, in beauty, and in righteousness, with singleness of heart as thy servants, and to the benefit of our fellow men."[17]

In her writings, Eleanor frequently stated that democracy required citizens to take interest in the well-being of their neighbors. These prayers show how the sentiments of the wider church correlated to her personal beliefs and the actions they inspired. A quick glance at hymns from the two hymnals in use for more than half her life (1916 and 1940) reveals even more correlations to concern for neighbors, generally, and for the disadvantaged, specifically. From the *Hymnal 1916*, a 1782 hymn by Charles Wesley (#505) prays, "Help us to help each other, Lord, each other's burdens bear; let each his friendly aid afford, to soothe another's care." Another from Emily V. Clark in 1891 (#503) sounds an incarnational theme: "We find thee where thou dwell'st below beside the beds of want and woe. . . . Be ours the hearts and hands to bless the sorrowing sons of wretchedness." Samuel Wolcott's 1869 hymn (#486) proclaims, "Christ for the world we sing! The world to Christ we bring, with loving zeal; the poor, and them that mourn, the faint and over-borne, sin-sick and sorrow worn, whom Christ doth heal."[18]

The "Fatherhood of God and the Brotherhood of Man" was a concept widely embraced by mainline Protestantism in the first half of the twentieth century. A hymn from 1910 by Charles H. Richards (#499) ends each verse with the phrase "the brotherhood of man." Frank Mason North's 1905 hymn (#494) laments the "cries of race and clan."

In the *Hymnal 1940*, John Oxenham's 1908 hymn "In Christ There Is No East or West" (#263), the third verse admonishes the people to, "Join hands, then, brothers of the faith, what-e'er your race may be! Who serves my Father as a son is surely kin to me." Labor concerns were also addressed. One hymn from Oxenham (#510) from 1920 affirms that "all labor gained new dignity since he who all creation made toiled with his hands for daily bread." The second verse asserts that "no work is commonplace, if all be done as unto him alone; life's simplest toil to him is known, who knoweth all." A longer and more theologically complex hymn from Henry van Dyke, whose meditation Eleanor carried in her purse, is the hymn "Jesus thou divine Companion" (#511). It contains the incarnational view: "Thou has come to join the workers, burden-bearers of the earth. Thou, the carpenter of Nazareth, toiling for thy daily food, by thy patience and thy courage, thou has taught us toil is good." The second verse adds, "Where the many toil together, there art thou among thine own." It concludes with "thou the peace that passeth knowledge, dwellest in the daily strife; thou the bread of heav'n, are broken in the sacrament of life."

Eleanor's lesson, learned over and over again, about staring down fear was also a factor in her ability to "stay in the fray." It is not difficult to imagine her lustily singing the words to Harry Emerson Fosdick's 1930 hymn "God of Grace and God of Glory" (#524), which ends the first verse with "grant us wisdom, grant us courage for the facing of this hour." The second verse prays "from the fears that long have bound us free our hearts to faith and praise," concluding with the recurring request for wisdom and courage "for the living of these days." Another petition, "Cure thy children's warring madness" resonated with Eleanor's previously noted pacifist inclinations.[19]

Beyond these elements, there were other factors from which she drew strength. From the time she entered the White House, she had the knowledgeable and reliable support of Lorena Hickok, to be sure, but she had older and deeper ties, not the least of whom was her husband. Not only had she been married to FDR for twenty-eight years at the start of the New Deal, but she had known him her entire life. Despite her frustration with his political reticence on matters such as the anti-lynching law, she had his tacit (albeit usually off-the-record) support for her advocacy on that and many other issues. Throughout his career (and hers), it was understood that she could often do things he himself could not do for political reasons but might actually support. For the most part, he made no attempt to restrain her, letting her take responsibility for her own actions. And, finally, there was what may have been the "secret sauce"—her charming, grandmotherly personality.

NONVIOLENT RESISTANCE, GRANNIE-STYLE

Eleanor's mother had nicknamed her daughter "Grannie" when she was still a toddler. By 1938, the fifty-four-year-old Eleanor had been a real grandmother for eleven years.

The Southern Conference for Human Welfare would provide an opportunity to demonstrate just what a charming grandmother can get away with.

The conference was meeting in the municipal auditorium in Birmingham, Alabama. Eleanor was expected to attend, but state law mandated racial segregation of the auditorium. Conference organizers took no chances. Not only were the segregated sections separated by a wide aisle, but pathways on the floor had been carefully marked so that speakers returning from the podium would not enter the wrong section by mistake. Commissioner of Public Safety Eugene Connor, known to one and all as "Bull," boasted that he would show the First Lady who was boss. He would arrest *any* white person who dared to cross the line, including the wife of the president of the United States.

In his account of the incident, Harold Ivan Smith said Eleanor's late arrival had led some to believe that she had decided not to attend, but when she entered the room, participants cheered. Eleanor acknowledged the applause then quickly took a seat on the aisle of the white section. Whatever disappointment (or satisfaction) the participants may have felt, inch by inch the First Lady made clear her position—literally. Some delegates noticed that the First Lady's chair had moved ever so slightly into the aisle. Then the chair moved again. Smith recounted, "Perhaps she felt crowded or could not see the podium. The chair moved again!" Slowly, the chair kept moving, prompting some participants to stand to get a better view. "By the end of the speaker's presentation, the First Lady sat in the middle of the wide aisle between the 'white only' and the 'Negro only' sections."[20] She had not broken the law, nor had she let Bull Connor have the last word. She had made no peace with oppression. In a graphic way, she had illustrated what Jesus advised. She had knowingly made herself vulnerable in a hostile context. She had turned the other cheek.

A DEEPENING COMMITMENT TO CIVIL RIGHTS

Having experienced the ferocity (and absurdity) of racial segregation, Eleanor's commitment to racial justice would only grow stronger as time went by. As noted earlier, she had committed to hiring black people for her household staff in the 1920s. At a conference in 1927, she had met the pioneering educator and Presbyterian activist Mary McLeod Bethune, a daughter of former slaves, who founded the school known today as Bethune-Cookman University. A lasting friendship developed, and Bethune would become the first black woman to head a federal agency when FDR appointed her to lead the National Youth Administration.

Eleanor's friendship with Walter White had also deepened in the years since she had joined the NAACP. But in the months after her Birmingham visit, she would become acquainted with a young woman whose work would influence not just Eleanor Roosevelt but also Thurgood Marshall, Ruth Bader Ginsberg, and the Episcopal Church. It all began with a letter but grew to include more than three hundred letters, supplemented with notes, birthday,

Christmas, sympathy, and get-well cards, and dozens of "clippings, reports, manuscripts, photographs, flowers, and candy."[21]

Discussions of labor and civil rights issues occurred over tea at the White House, or Eleanor's New York City apartments, or at Val-Kill. And the two of them formally worked together until the day Eleanor died. The remarkable woman who would become such a steadfast friend was Pauli Murray—educator, activist, lawyer, and ultimately the first black woman ordained to the Episcopal priesthood.

One explanation for the depth and duration of their friendship is that they had several things in common beyond their shared concern for social justice. Like Eleanor, Pauli had lost both of her parents at a young age. Eleanor was a devoted educator, having continued to teach young women at Todhunter School in New York throughout her husband's governorship. Pauli was from a family of educators, including her parents and grandparents, her sisters and brothers, and at least one aunt. Her grandfather had founded several schools under the auspices of the Freedmen's Bureau, and her father had been a principal in the Baltimore public school system. And they were both Episcopalians from "way back"—seven generations in Pauli's case.[22]

Their relationship began when Murray copied the First Lady on a somewhat angry letter she had sent the president. Murray included a separate cover letter to Eleanor. The presidential letter cycled through the proper channels and ultimately got a bureaucratic response a month later. Eleanor, however, responded personally within two weeks.

The letters were occasioned by a speech FDR had delivered that December at the University of North Carolina, where he was awarded an honorary doctorate. An estimated ten thousand people, segregated by race, heard the speech on site, while countless others, like Murray, heard it on network radio. The speech applauded the university's commitment to social progress and was well-received in many quarters, but not in the black press. Pauli Murray knew why. She had applied for admission for graduate study and was told black people were not admitted.

The First Lady's response was sympathetic but cautious, disappointing Pauli on the one hand but gratifying her by its personal nature. "The South is changing, but don't push too fast," Eleanor advised, but she herself did not take her own advice. Two days later in her "My Day" column, she asked her readers, "Are you free if you cannot vote, if you cannot be sure that the same justice will be meted out to you as to your neighbor; if you are expected to live on a lower level than your neighbor and to work for lower wages; if you are barred from certain places and opportunities?"[23]

The two continued to grow closer as they collaborated on various causes. Murray subsequently enrolled at historically black Howard University Law School, and despite the misgivings of professors who questioned why a woman would study law, she graduated first in her class in 1944. Eleanor Roosevelt could not attend the graduation because she was out of town, but she sent a bouquet from the president and herself.

During her last year of law school, Pauli had written a paper arguing that *Plessy v. Ferguson*, the Supreme Court case that justified "separate but equal," should be overturned because the doctrine it upheld "does violence to the individual." That, in fact, was the argument fellow Episcopalian Thurgood Marshall would make in his landmark case, *Brown v. Board of Education* ten years later.[24] Although he did not credit her work, he described her later work, *States' Laws on Race and Color*, as the "bible" for civil rights lawyers.[25]

As part of her graduation honors, Murray had been awarded the prestigious Rosenwald Fellowship, an honor bestowed on Marian Anderson, Langston Hughes, W. E. B. Du Bois, and Zora Neale Hurston. Murray's fellowship would enable her to pursue graduate study in labor law at Harvard Law School, where Howard sent all its outstanding law graduates. Unlike the University of North Carolina, Harvard Law had admitted black students as far back as 1860, and many of Howard's own professors were Harvard graduates. Nonetheless, Murray's (and Howard University's) hopes were dashed. Harvard Law School did not—and would not—admit women. Even a letter from FDR, a Harvard alumnus and sitting president of the United States, had no effect.[26]

Murray went on to study at the University of California and continued her correspondence and visits with Eleanor Roosevelt. In 1962, when President Kennedy asked Eleanor to chair his commission on the status of women, he named Murray to the commission on Eleanor's recommendation.

Although Eleanor did not live to see its completion, Murray drafted the final report giving Eleanor her due.

In 1971, future Supreme Court Justice Ruth Bader Ginsberg added Pauli Murray's name to her brief in the landmark case *Reed v. Reed*, which extended the Fourteenth Amendment's Equal Protection Clause to women for the first time. By this time, Pauli had become a tenured professor at Brandeis University, but like Eleanor, she was coming to the conclusion that most of the human rights problems the world struggled with were ultimately moral and spiritual problems. She shocked her friends and colleagues by giving up her position at Brandeis to enroll at the General Theological Seminary in New York, even though the Episcopal Church had not yet approved the ordination of women to the priesthood.[27]

By the time she graduated, however, ordination had been approved. After she was ordained in 1977, she returned to the Chapel of the Cross in Chapel Hill, North Carolina, to celebrate her first Eucharist. The chapel had special meaning for Pauli. It was where her grandmother had been baptized as a slave in 1858. In her Bible she carried a purple ribbon and dried flowers from the bouquet Eleanor had sent her thirty-three years before.[28]

CONTRADICTIONS AND CONSOLATIONS

The role of First Lady, which at one time seemed like a task "too hard" for Eleanor, nonetheless afforded her many opportunities to address, sometimes even remedy, the many social ills she cared about. Still there were times when nominal duties conflicted with heartfelt concerns. One year at Christmastime, she found herself in the ironic situation of visiting a newly christened battleship in the morning and then going to a local school's Christmas carol ceremony in the afternoon.

> At this season of the year, especially, it seems so irreconcilable that we should sing about the birth of a Baby who lived His life to bring greater happiness to man and died a willing sacrifice to prove that the law of love could outlive the law of hate, and yet, through all the centuries, continue to emphasize in our contacts with each other the law of force and hate! We must respect and admire and show our gratitude to those men in our fighting forces who protect us, but they must wish with us that the Christ Child's spirit could rule the world.[29]

Three months later, Easter would provide the occasion for yet another commentary on war and peace.

> Easter Day, in a world where a great number of men seem to be thinking of destruction, and the Resurrection of the Prince of Peace is celebrated. Some of His followers thought He had come to reign over an earthly kingdom. They found it hard to understand that He should die like a criminal in order that He could rise again within men's hearts and live through the ages as the personification of love and forgiveness. His way was the only way to peace among men. He charted a

The clergy of St. James', Hyde Park; Queen Elizabeth and King George VI of Great Britain; FDR and son James; the president's mother, Sara Delano Roosevelt; and First Lady Eleanor. Courtesy of FDR Library.

> way for the world but He has not as yet won His kingdom. It still exists only in the hearts of some people and the fight goes on. Every Easter we are reminded that it is possible to triumph over hate, greed and horror and that the Christ still lives and waits for His kingdom.[30]

Throughout the Washington years, Eleanor would channel this broad moral understanding into specific acts of kindness. She said she and FDR tried

> to maintain our family traditions as well as those that [had] been established in the White House. . . . Christmas Eve in Washington was usually a busy day for me. I started by going to a party for underprivileged children, given by the welfare council of the National Theater. Then I joined my husband to wish all the people in the executive offices a merry Christmas. Usually at lunchtime I had to be at the Salvation Army headquarters, where we had a service just before the food baskets were given out. I am afraid that during the depression years these services had an unchristian effect upon me, because invariably, before receiving their baskets, the poor wretches were told how grateful they should be. I knew if I were in their shoes, I would be anything but grateful. From there I went to the Volunteers of America for the same sort of service and giving of food baskets, returning home in time for the afternoon party in the East Room.[31]

The party was followed with the president's lighting of the community Christmas tree and the broadcast of his Christmas message. Then he would return home while Eleanor made her way to a Christmas tree in one of the poorer neighborhoods, where she joined in singing Christmas carols with the neighbors. Back at the White House after "the stockings had been filled, Miss Thompson [her secretary] and I nearly always went to midnight services at St. Thomas' Church."[32] The drive to Dupont Circle usually involved stops at the homes of families in some of Washington's poorest neighborhoods, where Eleanor would bring gifts and neighborly greetings.

Given her consistent emphasis on the needs of children, it is not surprising to learn that when war broke out in Europe, she established, with the president's blessing, the United States Committee for the Care of European Children. The purpose was to bring children from countries under siege or threat of siege to the United States for the duration of the war.

The president and First Lady return to St. Thomas' Church, Washington, D.C., where they had worshipped when FDR was assistant secretary of the Navy. He served on the vestry at that time. Photo courtesy of UPI. Used with permission.

STRONG COMMUNITIES EQUAL STRONG DEFENSE

As fears that the United States might be involved in a second European war increased, domestic politics shifted away from social policy to questions of "preparedness." Eleanor was concerned that New Deal priorities might be eclipsed by this new focus on war. One of the ways to prevent such a shift would be to insist that "preparedness" meant more than just matériel and military training. It meant strengthening the communities that would form the backbone of the home front. She had been inspired by the work of her English friend, Lady Stella Reading, who had organized Women's Voluntary Services for Civil Defense, which was credited with transforming the concept of civil defense into a force for social justice.[33]

She joined with other women in the administration in arguing that the social policy aims of the New Deal were more important than ever. The failure of almost a third of men to meet Army physical standards, she said, was a function of malnutrition and poor health care—concerns FDR himself had decried in his second inaugural address, in which he said he saw "one-third of a nation ill-housed, ill-clothed, ill-nourished." Barriers that prevented African Americans from working in defense industries had to be removed. A national health program was more important than ever. Rent controls and wage and price ceilings were needed to prevent profiteering, she argued.

Despite pressures from Congress to cut back on nutrition assistance in favor of military spending and despite opposition to "women's concerns" in his own cabinet, FDR made clear in his executive order creating the Office of Civilian Defense that it was to be a "social defense" organization. The organization would be responsible not just for civilian protection, volunteer participation, and maintenance of morale but also for securing the cooperation of all federal agencies to meet the needs of communities affected by defense programs.

By now, no one doubted Eleanor's impressive organizational skills. She had organized the first press conferences for women reporters in the Washington Press Corps, who were often shortchanged with opportunities for "scoops." She had also organized policy-focused White House conferences, and continued her work with the Democratic Party, faithfully writing her "My Day" columns, which had now become an institution. So it came as no surprise that she would have an office in the Dupont Circle headquarters of the Office of Civilian Defense. A meeting in her office to discuss the needs of children produced an interagency agreement, "no mean achievement" in Joseph Lash's words, on a program of federal support for daycare and additional grants to the states for maternal health, child health, and child welfare services.[34]

Eleanor worked tirelessly in this new role, but in September of 1941, she faced two more personal challenges. Her mother-in-law died at the beginning of the month, and her brother Hall at the end. Less than three months later, the Japanese would attack Pearl Harbor. When that fateful day occurred and it was clear that war could not be avoided, Eleanor faced it with resignation. In a radio broadcast, she said: "For months now the knowledge that something of this kind might happen has been hanging over our heads, and yet it seemed impossible to believe, impossible to drop the everyday things of life and feel that there was only one thing which was important, and that was preparation to meet an enemy, no matter where he struck. That is all over now and there is no more uncertainty. We know what we have to face and we know that we are ready to face it."[35]

She was already familiar with the devastation of the war. Beautiful places she had visited on her early European trips lay in ruins as she joined Franklin on a post-armistice tour as part of his job in the Wilson Administration. She had seen the traumatized and disabled soldiers in the hospitals she had visited. She had seen enough of war to convince her that war as an instrument of policy, war as a means of settling disputes, was immoral. As noted earlier, throughout the interwar years she had worked with groups such as the Women's International League for Peace and Freedom. Now she was about to gain even more knowledge firsthand.

At the time of America's entrance into the war, Eleanor was already in the habit of extensive travel, both in pursuit of her own cherished causes as well as an ambassador of the administration and a valuable set of eyes and ears for the president. It is estimated that she logged in excess of forty thousand miles of travel each year, a record that would soon be broken.

Eleanor with the troops in the South Pacific. The First Lady insisted on dining with the enlisted men rather than with the officers. Courtesy of FDR Library.

Flying under an assumed name, she made a secret passage across the Atlantic to visit Great Britain. Landing in Ireland, she was secreted to England and placed on board a train for Paddington Station, where she was met by King George VI and Queen Elizabeth.[36] She, of course, knew them well from their famous visit to New York, where she treated them to hot dogs at Hyde Park and took them to church at St. James'. All told, she spent a month there, seeing the success of Lady Reading's work in civil defense and visiting US troops stationed there. In characteristic fashion, she declined to sit at the officers' tables for meals, preferring to eat elbow-to-elbow with the enlisted men.

Her visit was considered so successful in bolstering morale, even Winston Churchill commented on her "golden footprints." Less than a year later, when she stepped into the cage-style wood paneled elevator with Franklin to ride up to the family quarters at the White House, he suggested she should make a trip to Australia, New Zealand, and the Pacific Islands. She enthusiastically responded, "When?"[37]

The top secret mission was arranged for the fall of 1942. Eleanor dutifully churned out ten "My Day" columns datelined Hyde Park in advance to prevent the news media from noticing her absence. Once on the ground, she donned a Red Cross uniform and dutifully made inspections of hospitals, but she wanted to visit the troops on the frontlines of Guadalcanal, where the Allies had successfully launched the first major offensive against the Japanese. Permission was originally denied, but when Admiral William Halsey saw the effect of her hospital visits, he concluded that the boost in morale was worth the extra precautions that would be needed to safeguard the First Lady. He noted that her visits were not just perfunctory meetings with hospital officials. She visited every ward, stopped at every bed, spoke to every patient, and offered to convey messages back home. She dutifully logged the name of each patient and the injuries sustained, as well the name and address of the loved one to be contacted.

From the front lines, she wrote to FDR about the effects of shell shock (now called post-traumatic stress disorder).

He, in turn, ordered more frequent rest and rotation and other humane measures for the troops.

"On Guadalcanal, as in many other places, I said a prayer in my heart for the growth of the human spirit so that we might do away with force in settling disputes in the future," she wrote in her diary.[38] Little did she know that she would one day be asked to help build the mechanisms for that hope.

Her prayer "for the growth of the human spirit" was rather typical of the way she prayed. She did not believe you could or should ask God to give you things you merely desired, like a puppy or a prom date. She believed God primarily bestowed gifts of *character*, such as strength, courage, patience, and the ability to understand and appreciate others. She also believed God would protect against complacency, fretfulness, and self-pity. All of these character attributes were mentioned in her nightly prayer and can also be inferred from the Prayer of St. Francis. A prayer for "growth of the human spirit" is essentially a prayer for character development for the human race as a whole.

In 1929, an Episcopalian by the name of Frank Billings Kellogg, who had been appointed secretary of state by President Calvin Coolidge, won the Nobel Peace Prize for his successful work with French Foreign Minister Aristide Briand to develop the Kellogg-Briand Pact. Ultimately signed by thirty-one nations, the pact renounced the use of war to resolve disputes. While it is widely regarded by historians as a failure because it did not prevent World War

II, it accomplished something very significant. It created the legal (and moral) foundation for holding individuals accountable for war crimes and crimes against humanity.

Amid the jubilation of the war's end, the Allies began deliberations lasting through the summer of 1945 to establish a mechanism for accountability. They agreed to create an international tribunal to try the surviving Nazi leadership. The tribunal would meet in Nuremberg, located in the American occupation zone, which was the site of the most significant Nazi rallies.

Eleanor supported the trials, not for the sake of retribution, but to affirm that love is stronger than hate. As the trials got underway, she commented:

> I heard, the other day, of a country where some of the people look upon the Nuremberg trial as a joke and think that all they hear about the horrors of concentration camps is pure propaganda. I hope there is no one left in our own country who is so willfully blind and deaf as these people are reported to be. It is only by acknowledging that human beings, when they once accept wrong leadership, can be led far astray that we can guard ourselves from ever accepting it.
>
> We must remember that the hope of the world lies in acceptance of a philosophy which has come down to us through the ages. Love can be stronger than hate, but we as individuals have to see to it that love and not hate is the basis of our action.[39]

The next chapter of her life would be devoted to creating a new world order based on respect for human dignity. Respect, as it has often been said, is the minimal face of love.

CHAPTER SIX

SHOW US A VISION OF A WORLD MADE NEW

"[Y]OU CAN NEVER KNOW how terribly frightened I was when I got on that ship that night to go to London. I came to the ship alone, and I was simply terrified. I felt that I was going to do a job that I knew nothing about. I knew I did not know anything about it . . ."[1] Eleanor Roosevelt wrote these words recalling the beginning of a chapter in her life that would be an unanticipated answer to both her nightly prayer and her beloved Prayer of St. Francis. She would indeed be shown a vision of a world made new, and she would also become an instrument of God's peace. The woman standing alone at the ship, carrying her own bags as usual, was embarking on a journey that would have lasting global implications.

This confession of fear was addressed to Virginia Stettinius, whose husband, the former secretary of state, Edward

Stettinius Jr., had been assigned by the state department to advise Mrs. Roosevelt as she undertook her work on behalf of the United Nations. Similar to being First Lady, it was a job she had never sought, a job she thought she could not do.

"And the angel said unto her, Fear not, Mary: for thou hast found favour with God."[2] Eleanor, no doubt, had memorized that verse and taught it to others in her youth. Yet like Mary, she was deeply troubled when crossing the many thresholds of life. She dreaded being a debutante, yet she managed to do it and do it on her own terms. She minimized her attendance at the endless round of required parties and embraced Mary Harriman's Junior League vision of debutantes who give to the community through settlement house work. Even though she was fearful of entering tenements and fearful of being on the streets of the Lower East Side unescorted, it was her choice, and she never backed away from it.

At another threshold, she was overcome with grief at the thought of being First Lady, yet nine months after moving into the White House, she published her first book, *It's Up to the Women*, in which she urged working women to demand equal pay for equal work and to join unions or organize new ones.[3] She asked wealthy women to treat the people who worked for them with respect, offering decent wages and working conditions. She began her "My Day" column reporting on the things she learned and what she believed needed to be done.

Soon after that, unlike any First Lady before or since, it appeared as though she had thumbed her nose at fear.

At the Willow Grove mine in Ohio, she flashed reporters a grin as bright as the light on her coal miner's cap and descended two miles underground. Sitting in the front of a six-car train, she watched the miners work and listened to a local union leader explain the mine operations. Then, deeper into the mine, she got out of the car and talked with individual miners about their wages, working conditions, safety precautions, and mining methods.[4]

She had figured out how to be a First Lady on her own terms, but it was also taking a toll. Her triumphant visit to Guadalcanal had resulted in the loss of thirty pounds from her trim frame and triggered a deep depression alleviated only by the constant press of official duties.[5]

Then in April 1945, just as World War II was coming to an end with an Allied victory assured, President Roosevelt died at his retreat in Warm Springs, Georgia. The whole nation plunged into mourning the death of its longest-serving president. Eleanor immediately made her way to Georgia to accompany the funeral train back to Washington. The president's casket was in the same car he and Eleanor used on his many train trips around the country. Thousands turned out at each stop along the way to present wreaths and have a moment of reflection. When the train reached Washington, the casket was transported by a horse-drawn caisson to the White House. After a small funeral service in the East Room led by the Rt. Rev. Angus Dun, bishop of Washington, the casket was transported back to the train to make its way to Hyde Park for the main funeral and burial.

One hour before the president's funeral, millions tuned in to the NBC Radio Network to hear the celebrated contralto Betty Spain sing a solemn memorial accompanied by the famed NBC Symphony Orchestra led by Arturo Toscanini.[6] All of America, in its religious, civic, and commercial guises was in mourning.

Despite her personal grief at the end of a forty-year marriage, which had yielded five children and some twenty grandchildren, along with unprecedented opportunities to serve the public and advocate social justice, duty required Eleanor Roosevelt to take on yet another role she had not sought. Eleanor was expected to be mourner-in-chief, not only for the countless people who had served in the nation's longest presidential administration, but ultimately for the nation as a whole.

And if all this were not enough, she faced the daunting task of vacating the White House after a twelve-year tenure and the possibly even more daunting task of settling her husband's substantial estate. The last thing she wanted to think about was taking on a new project. She already had one. Yet it seemed as if the whole country had ideas about what she should do next. Through her newspaper column and many groundbreaking activities as First Lady, she had become both well-known and widely admired. People knew what she was capable of doing. After all the unprecedented activities as First Lady, her public seemed to want more. Recommendations to seek public office poured in. She was besieged with offers to head women's colleges, and many other high profile jobs were suggested. But Eleanor was seriously pondering the question of whether the time had come to settle into private life after twenty-five years on the public stage. As the matriarch of a large and increasingly distinguished family, she would have plenty to keep her busy.

AN INSTRUMENT OF PEACE

And then the call came from recently inaugurated President Harry Truman. He wanted to appoint Eleanor to the US delegation to the newly formed United Nations. The principal organizing conference in San Francisco had occurred, with Truman's blessing, only four days after President Roosevelt died. The following August, President Truman authorized the atomic bombing of Hiroshima and Nagasaki. By September, Japan had surrendered. The hope for world peace was frighteningly frail. Yet, with Truman's overture, Eleanor was being asked to do something that she had long prayed for: to be an instrument of peace.

She did not feel up to the task. "How could I be a delegate to help organize the United Nations when I have no background or experience in international meetings?" she asked the president. Truman was convinced that her real-world, person-to-person experience was more than adequate. As Eleanor most likely realized, Truman also had no background or experience with international meetings. Still, his confidence in her persuaded her to accept.[7] Clearly God was answering her prayer to be kept at tasks that demanded her best efforts. And she was being driven to God for strength.

In January of 1946, only nine months after her husband had died, she set sail on that lonely voyage to London. From aboard the ship, she wrote to her daughter, asking her to say "prayers that I am really useful in this job for I feel very inadequate."[8]

By all accounts, Anna's prayers were answered in the affirmative. In the view of Harvard Law professor Mary Ann Glendon, Eleanor Roosevelt's crowning achievement, the Universal Declaration of Human Rights, far exceeded expectations:

> In the years that followed, to the astonishment of many, human rights would become a political factor that not even the most hard-shelled realist could ignore. The Universal Declaration would become an instrument, as well as the most prominent symbol, of changes that would amplify the voices of the weak in the corridors of power. It challenged the long-standing view that a sovereign state's treatment of its own citizens was that nation's business and no one else's. It gave expression to diffuse, deep-seated longings and lent wings to movements that would soon bring down colonial empires. Its thirty concise articles inspired or influenced scores of postwar and postcolonial constitutions and treaties, including the new constitutions of Germany, Japan, and Italy. It became the polestar of an army of international human rights activists, who pressure governments to live up to their pledges and train the searchlight of publicity on abuses that would have remained hidden in

> former times. Confirming the worst fears held in 1948 by the Soviet Union and South Africa, the Declaration provided a rallying point for the freedom movements that spurred the collapse of totalitarian regimes in Eastern Europe and the demise of apartheid. It is the parent document, the primary inspiration, for most rights instruments in the world today.[9]

There is a passage in the Gospel according to Luke in which Jesus assures his disciples that, at the moment of trial, he will give them "words and a wisdom" that none of their opponents will be able to withstand or contradict (Luke 21:15). Something along those lines seems to have happened to Eleanor Roosevelt as she learned to deal graciously with the less-than-cooperative attitudes of her Soviet colleagues and the initial hostility of the Republican members of her own delegation.

She seems to have gotten her stride early on. Even while preoccupied with the aftermath of her husband's death the previous July, she still had found time to read the freshly drafted United Nations Charter and to comment favorably on it in her "My Day" column. Her friend, Mary McLeod Bethune, had participated in drafting the Charter, the only black woman to do so. The preamble lays out the purposes of the new international body: "To save succeeding generations from the scourge of war, which twice in our lifetime has brought untold sorrow to mankind, and to reaffirm faith in fundamental human rights, in the dignity and worth of the human person, in the equal rights of men and women and of nations large and small, and to establish conditions under which justice and respect for the obligations arising from treaties and other sources of international law can be maintained, and to promote social progress and better standards of life in larger freedom . . ."[10]

The preamble goes on to assert that "for these ends to practice tolerance and live together in peace with one another as good neighbours, and to unite our strength to maintain international peace and security, and to ensure, by the acceptance of principles and the institution of methods, that armed force shall not be used, save in the common interest, and to employ international machinery for the promotion of the economic and social advancement of all peoples . . ."

The text could have been written by Eleanor Roosevelt herself given that it so closely paralleled what she had stood for throughout her life. In a March 1946 column, she shared some of the thinking behind the concept for the new organization:

> Instead of running an armament race against each other and building up trade cartels and political alliances, we the nations of the world should join together each contributing a certain amount of military strength to be used only against an aggressor. We would use the forum of the United Nations to discuss our difficulties and our grievances using our diplomatic machinery to adjust such things as we could among ourselves, but bringing questions that individual governments disagreed on before the bar of the United Nations as a whole. Difficult machinery to work out, but it aims at the nations of the

> world living under law, using an international court of justice and only resorting to force to curb an aggressor.[11]

A formal statement about human rights was not actually on anybody's mind, but when the various committees began their work, it was recognized that if the UN were to promote respect for human rights, there would need to be some agreement on what the term actually meant. Eventually, Eleanor would be elected to chair the drafting of what became the Universal Declaration of Human Rights. Over the next two years, she would hold her colleagues' feet to the fire to assure the drafting of a document that lived up to the lofty ideals of the preamble.

The Lebanese philosopher and statesman Charles Habib Malik, who succeeded her as chair of the Human Rights Commission, took the occasion of the twentieth anniversary of the Universal Declaration to reflect on Eleanor's role in its creation: "President Roosevelt bequeathed to mankind the legacy of his Four Freedoms, which we had at the back of our mind all the time. Through her very name Mrs. Roosevelt imported this legacy into our council chambers. But she brought to her task as a leader and colleague much more than this: she brought a distinguished personality, an outstanding charm and dignity, a deep personal concern for all conditions of men and for all matters affecting human rights. These qualities were transparent in all her attitudes and statements, and they were contagious among our ranks. Were it not for her leadership in those years . . . I doubt that our work would have been crowned with success as early as 1948."[12]

THE HOSPITALITY SOLUTION

Malik himself was the intended object of some of that charm. Glendon expands on Eleanor's somewhat disingenuous description of tea in her Greenwich Village apartment with Malik and China's Peng-chun Chang, the two leading intellectuals on the Human Rights Commission. John Humphrey, the Canadian director of the UN's Human Rights Division was also present.

"As we settled down over the teacups," Eleanor said in her 1958 autobiography *On My Own*, "one of them made a remark with philosophical implications, and a heated discussion ensued." She described Dr. Chang as a pluralist who "held forth in charming fashion on the proposition that there is more than one kind of ultimate reality." Malik—a Roman Catholic—appealed to the philosophy of Thomas Aquinas in response. She said the conversation became "so lofty" that she had difficulty following it. "So I simply filled the teacups again and sat back to be entertained by the talk of these learned gentlemen."[13]

Once again, Eleanor had turned to the "hospitality solution" that had worked so well in so many different ways in the past. Glendon said none of the guests "would have taken this archly modest account at face value. They were already familiar with her style of chairmanship, in which she did, indeed, 'sit back' and let everyone have his or her say—all the while studying how to steer the discussion toward her desired outcome.

"What she did not mention in her autobiography," Glendon says, "but what the U.N. record shows, is that bickering between Chang and Malik, who had emerged as intellectual leaders on the commission, was threatening to become a problem. In such cases it was not her style to take people to the woodshed; instead, she invited them to tea. Although the arguments between the two never completely ceased, Roosevelt did succeed in getting them to work together effectively on the all-important drafting committee."[14]

Tea worked other miracles too. Although she and Hansa Mehta of India were the only women on the commission, there were quite a few women in other capacities at the various UN meetings. Eleanor began inviting them to tea as well, providing encouragement and organizational incentives for them just as she had done for the women in the Washington press corps years earlier.

Tea wasn't the secret ingredient though. It was her deep appreciation of relationality. Women traditionally are understood as having a unique role in the formation of relationships, but in Eleanor's case, there was a moral dimension as well stemming from her participation in a religious tradition that emphasized right relationship rather than "right belief." While it may start with family, it grows to be universal.

In a Christmas Day column one year, she expanded on what was one of her main understandings of the faith:

> The whole Christmas story I believe, emphasizes the value of family and the family relationship. . . . The family is closely knit together to emphasize the fact that they are

not just single individuals, but interdependent and the failures or successes of each are shared by all.

Gradually we are learning that this story that began to be taught to us by the birth of a baby so many centuries ago, and the traditions which that life brought into the world, are now broadening into the interdependence of nations. If we believe that where men of pure heart do their work in the world, it results in the developing gradually of a pattern which is part of a master plan, then we must believe that those things which have tended to draw nations closer together to bring us more intercommunication in thought and in physical contact, must be used to develop the kind of human beings and that way of life which the great spiritual teachers of the world have preached in different parts of the world. Our lessons have come to us from the life of Christ. Great numbers of people take theirs from the teachings of Mohammet or Budda or some other prophet, but in almost every case these are the teachers and the one God gives up to the opportunity to follow His plan. We fail and struggle but each year for those of us who are Christians, on Christmas Day with the birth of Christ we renew our faith and our hopes. We can wipe out the past, we can begin again. We can pledge ourselves anew to follow the teachings of Christ, to live as nearly as we can as He bade us live in love and charity towards our neighbor and in devotion to God. We can hear again the Angels announcing His coming to the shepherds as they watched their flocks and to the three Great Kings of the Orient, and with this same faith and humility they showed, we can rejoice in the birth of a child who taught us love by living and dying for all of mankind.[15]

CAUSES FOR HOPE

The quest for world peace and respect for human rights was gaining ground in the United States and around the world in 1948, the year the Declaration was finally approved by the UN. The year began with a call from Pope Pius XII to ban the atom bomb. Also in January, Alfred Kinsey would issue his groundbreaking report *Sexual Behavior in the Human Male*, which established that male homosexuality was far more widespread than anyone had previously thought, precipitating the formation of a wave of postwar civil rights organizations for gay men and lesbians.

With the shocking revelations of the Holocaust fresh in the public mind, the motion picture *Gentlemen's Agreement*, a film about antisemitism in polite society, won the Academy Award for best picture. Elia Kazan won for best director, and Celeste Holm won for best supporting actress. Similar acclaim was bestowed by the Golden Globes, the New York Film Critics Circle, and other bodies.

John Foster Dulles, who would become secretary of state in the Eisenhower Administration, called for a nationwide ban on employment discrimination based on race, religion, or national origin at a speech before the National Council for a Permanent Fair Employment Practice Commission.

In Greenwich Village, where Eleanor was living at the time, the local chapter of the American Veterans Committee announced a plan to boycott bars in the Village that discriminated against African Americans. The plan was supported by the Civil Rights Congress, the Tenants and Consumers Council, the Italian American Labor Council, and the American Jewish Congress. The latter organization also issued a comprehensive report on the status of antidiscrimination law in the United States. The report catalogued two hundred separate laws on the books at the state level banning various forms of discrimination based on race, religion, and national origin. Many were aimed at specific problems, such as exclusion from amusement parks, discrimination in the sale of cemetery plots, and the like. Others tackled employment and housing discrimination, but none took the form of the comprehensive bans that would come in the 1950s and 60s.

President Truman announced the desegregation of the armed forces and the federal workforce. He also issued an executive order prohibiting discrimination against the handicapped throughout the federal government.

Later in the year, New York Governor Thomas Dewey signed a law barring racial and religious discrimination in admissions to the state's colleges and universities, and the New York Academy of Medicine advanced a proposal to admit physicians to the American Medical Association regardless of race.

The Supreme Court of New Jersey anticipated *Brown v. Board of Education* by six years, ordering desegregation of New Jersey's public schools. Eleanor had previously applauded the town of Freehold, New Jersey, which had voluntarily desegregated its schools earlier in the year. Also in New Jersey, the Congress of Industrial Organizations called on the governor and two other state officials to bar the American Bowling Congress from holding a whites-only bowling competition in Atlantic City's civic auditorium. While the meeting was allowed to go forward, the congress subsequently opened membership to both African Americans and women.

One group that Eleanor had worked with directly, the United Council of Churchwomen, called for federal aid to education and the expansion of Social Security. It further declared that segregation and discrimination were contrary to Christian principles and inimical to the democratic way of life. Four years earlier, Eleanor had involved the group in a White House Conference on "How Women May Share in Post-War Policy-Making."[16]

As summer rolled around, the Republican Party at its national convention reiterated its support for civil rights legislation and called for statehood for Puerto Rico. Meanwhile, the Democrats included the first-ever civil rights plank in their platform, prompting Eleanor's longtime antagonist, Bull Connor, to lead a "Dixiecrat" walkout of Southern delegates. The States' Rights Party they formed caused the election to be so close that the *Chicago Tribune* prematurely called the election for Thomas Dewey. The famous photo of a grinning Harry Truman holding up a newspaper with the blazing headline "Dewey Defeats Truman" followed.

CHALLENGES TO PEACE

Truman's victory had significant consequences for Eleanor. Had the Republicans won, she might not have been able to continue in what had now become an extremely important role. But the threat of a sudden change in leadership was not the only problem threatening a global commitment to human rights. In May, David Ben Gurion proclaimed the formation of the State of Israel on the day the British mandate in Palestine ended. Although the UN General Assembly had called for the creation of two states, the Arab Palestinians rejected the proposal and enlisted the aid of neighboring Arab states to attack Israel. In the ensuing violence, many Palestinians were driven from their homes.

In Asia, civil war raged in China, and the occupation zones in Korea formed separate governments, setting the stage for what would be a full-blown war two years later.

The Cold War was deepening. In Germany, Allied plans to merge their occupation zones into an independent Federal Republic of West Germany had angered the Soviets to the point where they blockaded supply lines to the Allied occupation zones in Berlin. The Allies responded with an airlift, risking armed conflict with the Soviet Union.

The South African parliament voted to implement a formal program of racial segregation known as apartheid. Nearly two million people in India-Pakistan had died the year before. In 1948, the people would see their world-renowned apostle of nonviolence, Mohandas Ghandi, felled by an assassin's bullet.

Back home, a report of the New York State Legislature found that age discrimination in employment ran rampant and was widely defended. Some 39 percent of employers had formal rules barring the hiring of older workers. And there was yet another lynching in Georgia.

The stakes could not have been higher. A global commitment to human rights was needed more than ever. The hope for peace and the role she was playing to advance it was never far from Eleanor's mind. Her Easter column that year had said:

> St. John, in describing Christ's appearance to the disciples, records His salutation: "Peace Be Unto You," and when He appeared to them again to quiet the unbelief of Thomas the doubting one, He said: "Because thou hast seen me thou hast believed; blessed are they that have not seen and yet believed."
>
> It is hard for us to believe in peace and to keep our spirit keyed to the assurance that we can achieve the realization of Christ's words. We have not seen peace and yet we must believe in it, for without that belief in the thing which we seek and in our ability to find it, we will be as useless as the doubting disciple.
>
> Easter is the season that emphasizes for all of us the need for faith—faith in our religion, faith in ourselves, faith in our neighbors and in our friends and in the peoples of the world. If the United States has

Eleanor Roosevelt carrying her suitcase at LaGuardia Airport, New York, New York. Lawrence W. Jordan. Courtesy of FDR Library.

a destiny—and we Americans have believed this ever since the days of the Founding Fathers—then it would look as though the resolving of our difficulties at this time lies in greater faith—to insure greater effort toward the ultimate achievement for all upon earth of Christ's salutation: "Peace Be Unto You."[17]

Eleanor with Bishop William Scarlett of Missouri, who chaired the Federal Council of Churches Commission on a Just and Durable Peace, one of the first voices to call for what became the United Nations. Eleanor contributed a chapter to his anthology Christianity Takes a Stand, *published in 1946 by the church's Joint Commission on Social Reconstruction, which he chaired. Photo reprinted by permission of The Archives of the Episcopal Church.*

HOME FOR CHRISTMAS

Toward the end of the year, a draft declaration was nearing completion. With a strong desire to be back home in time to spend Christmas with her family, Eleanor pressed the committee to keep working, so much so that some members teasingly referred to her as their slave driver. Nonetheless, they kept working and the Declaration was ready to be submitted to the General Assembly. Eleanor's beloved niece (Hall's daughter) recounted how her aunt celebrated the milestone:

> On the day in December when the commission finally finished its work . . . Aunt Eleanor gave a small reception for her colleagues at the Palais des Nations in Geneva. She wrote to me that after all the guests had left and she was walking through the empty halls with her advisor, she came up with a better way to celebrate than with a glass of champagne at a party. The marble floors were polished to the shine of black ice. My aunt's feet were long and narrow, and her low-heeled shoes had leather soles. She ran, gathering momentum, and then slid down the hall, her arms outstretched in triumph. It was so much fun that she did it again.

On December 10, 1948, she continued, "Aunt Eleanor stood before a plenary session of the General Assembly of the United Nations and read the Universal Declaration of Human Rights, so painstakingly hammered out by her commission. It was unanimously accepted. Then the assembly did something it had never done before. Everyone rose to honor the speaker. This particular speaker had been able to put together a document that few thought was possible, and, not only that, it was a woman who had done it."[18]

WHAT THE UNIVERSAL DECLARATION ACCOMPLISHED

The Universal Declaration of Human Rights recognizes and defines a broader range of rights than those mentioned in Magna Carta, the English Bill of Rights of 1689, the American Declaration of Independence, the US Constitution and Bill of Rights, and the French Declaration of the Rights of Man and of the Citizen. Although it has been criticized as Western in origin and tone, the Declaration has a legitimate claim to universality because non-Westerners, including representatives of all the world's major religions, participated in its formulation.

The Declaration itself is not a law but a philosophical statement; in fact, the world's most widely agreed ethical statement about how human beings ought to treat one another. It calls on all individuals and all "organs of society" to promote respect for the rights and freedoms enumerated in the Declaration. It is different from the American Bill of Rights in that it is not framed as individual claims upon the government. It is framed as the claim of all human beings on all other human beings. It looks to the government to

Eleanor displays the first copy of the Universal Declaration of Human Rights. It was the crowning achievement of her work as chair of the UN Commission on Human Rights. Courtesy of FDR Library.

enforce or otherwise realize the rights, but they are not granted or conferred by governments.

Instead, it recognizes the rights as "inherent," stopping short of declaring them "God-given." A specific reference to a supreme being or to nature was ruled out to accommodate polytheistic and nontheistic religious perspectives. Eleanor herself said she would have preferred a reference to a supreme being, but she realized that if it were to be truly universal, it would have to be noncommittal about the source of rights. The Declaration simply says people are born with them.

Among the rights that were especially important to Eleanor was the language in the declaration guaranteeing freedom from discrimination of any kind, "such as race, colour, sex, language, religion, political or other opinion, national or social origin, property, birth or other status."[19] The inclusion of "other status" assured that forms of discrimination that might have been uncommon (or unheard of) at the time would still be covered. Age, disability, sexual orientation, and gender identity are examples. Two other articles reiterate the concept of freedom from discrimination, including the concept that people are to be free from "incitements" to discriminate against them.

The Declaration's discussion of religion was not limited to concerns about discrimination. While the US Bill of Rights affirms the "free exercise" of religion, the Universal Declaration upholds freedom of thought, conscience, and religion. Article 18 asserts that the right includes freedom for individuals to change their religion or belief, and "freedom, either alone or in community with others and in public or private," to manifest their religion or belief in "teaching, practice, worship, and observance."

The drafting of the article on religion and conscience benefited from the participation of American religious leaders in two ways. The first was the experience of religious pluralism in the United States where no church or other religious group had ever had a majority, even in colonial times. The second was the experience of American missionaries overseas.

The high degree of religious pluralism in the United States required a public discourse, so fully evident in Eleanor Roosevelt's writings, that acknowledged people might be of many different faiths or none at all. Individual conscience had to be respected. The right to change one's religion, taken for granted in the United States, was anything but assured in many countries of the world as many missionaries had learned. In many cases, if conversion were permitted, it may be accompanied by legal disabilities and prohibitions of public expression.[20]

Eleanor, with her extensive knowledge of the Bible, was quite likely aware that the story of what is believed to be the first known charter of human rights is found in the book of Ezra (1:1, KJV), which tells us that "the Lord stirred up the spirit of Cyrus king of Persia, that he made a proclamation throughout all his kingdom and put it also in writing. . . ." This proclamation, inscribed on a clay cylinder in Babylonian cuneiform, was discovered by archaeologists in 1879. It sets out a policy of religious toleration and promotes the material well-being of conquered peoples. The original Cyrus Cylinder resides in the British Museum. A replica commands a place of honor in the United Nations headquarters in New York.

Also important to Eleanor were the rights that have come to be known collectively as economic and social rights. The United States proposed their inclusion from the outset, a fact some will find astounding, given that the United States has been increasingly antagonistic toward them ever since.[21] They essentially embrace what FDR had presented to the American public in his last term as an "economic bill of rights." They include the right to work, the right to just and favorable conditions of work, protection against unemployment, equal pay for equal work, and just and favorable remuneration sufficient to maintain a family at a standard worthy of human dignity. Also included is the right to form and join trade unions; the right to rest and leisure; the right to food, clothing, housing, and medical care; and the right to security in the event of sickness, disability, widowhood, old age, or other lack of livelihood. Virtually all these concerns had been endorsed in myriad General Convention resolutions from the time of Eleanor's birth. They had also enjoyed the support of other mainline denominations in the United States, as well as the Roman Catholic Church from the time of Pope Leo XIII.

Contemporary commentators frequently refer to the economic and social rights as "new rights," meaning that they first received legal articulation in the nineteenth and twentieth centuries, whereas such rights as freedom of speech stemmed from the eighteenth century. Eleanor shared this view and even described them as stemming from the necessities of the Industrial Revolution. However, the sixth-century Babylonian Talmud articulates a number of economic rights, such as the right to form trade unions, limits on hours of work, the right to eat, and the right to sick and disability pay, among others. Other rights can be inferred from Leviticus and Deuteronomy and elsewhere in the Bible.[22]

Yet despite this religious pedigree and the initial backing of the US government, the United States today is the only major nation that has not ratified the International Covenant on Economic, Social, and Cultural Rights, the multination treaty that establishes the Declaration's economic and social rights in international law. The reason is largely due to the beginnings of a Cold War between the Soviet Union and the West and the harsh anticommunism of the ensuing "McCarthy Era," which had counterparts in other parts of the world. For many years, most of America's Western allies had declined to ratify the covenant. Eleanor's committee had originally thought one covenant for all the provisions of the Declaration would be the appropriate course, but she resigned herself to the realities of the Cold War. She was disappointed but continued to champion the Declaration and the United Nations. Ultimately all but her own country came round to her way of thinking, although she did not live to see it. By 1976, the UN announced that a sufficient number of nations had ratified both covenants, enabling the UN to proclaim the International Bill of Rights. The announcement received little in attention in the United States, where bicentennial celebrations overshadowed a major world development.

An additional right was also included in the Declaration, one especially important to Eleanor as an educator: A right to education directed toward the promotion of understanding, tolerance, and friendship among all nations, racial, or religious groups. Eleanor's commitment to tolerance had grown more profound as she confronted her own prejudices.

In a 1918 letter to her mother-in-law, she had given voice to some negative stereotypes about Jews,[23] and when she became co-owner of the Todhunter School, she favored limiting the number of Jewish students, saying the spirit of the school would be very different if it had "too many" Jewish children.[24]

Beginning in the nineteen thirties, having become close to Jewish activists such as Rose Schneiderman, she became an increasingly vocal critic of antisemitism in Europe and the United States. In the wake of the Holocaust, she became a strong supporter of the quest for a Jewish homeland. She supported the US recognition of the newly formed state of Israel in 1948 and made several trips to Israel over the course of the next decade.

Eleanor's commitment to toleration extended to those who did not believe, as she did, that human rights come from God. She explained to an American audience why there is no reference to God or a Supreme Being in the Declaration. "Now I happen to believe that we are born free and equal in dignity and rights because there is a divine Creator, and there is a divine spark in men. But there were other people around the table who wanted it expressed in such a way that they could think in their particular way about this question."[25]

The final document simply declares, "All human beings are born free and equal in dignity and rights."[26] Even without a reference to God, all the world's major religions endorsed it. While the Declaration was still in draft, the 1948 Lambeth Conference of the world's Anglican bishops endorsed the proposed document in one resolution and spelled out specific concerns in others (racial discrimination, economic security, religious freedom, etc.). Anglican concern for human rights has had a long history. In 1215, Archbishop of Canterbury Stephen Langton drafted the Magna Carta, the great charter of freedom of the English people.

In the Episcopal Church, support for a United Nations was addressed in *The Living Church* in 1942 and followed by almost annual pronouncements from General Convention and church headquarters. In 1949, the General Convention issued a ringing endorsement of the Declaration and directed the Department of Christian Social Relations to prepare study materials for use throughout the church.[27]

One of the leaders in these various efforts was Eleanor's friend, Bishop William Scarlett of Missouri, who chaired the church's Joint Commission on Social Reconstruction. He was successful in persuading Eleanor to contribute a chapter to his anthology, *Christianity Takes a Stand*, which included contributions on social issues from Frances Perkins, Walter Russell Bowie, Angus Dun, Reinhold Niebuhr, and others. Eleanor's article dealt with the rights of minorities and insisted that it was wrong to make generalizations about groups. Loving your neighbor meant loving individual people, she said.[28]

Some biographers suggest that Eleanor's commitment to tolerance grew out of her encounter with other peoples through her UN work. But family testimony suggests that it was there well before that time. In fact, her nightly prayer asked God to open our hearts "to the loveliness men hide from us because we do not try to understand them."

Her grandson, Curtis Roosevelt (Dall), who lived in the White House, said there was not much discussion of religion in the family. "One's religious feelings and affiliations were considered private. If occasionally I overhead the labels 'atheist' or 'agnostic,' I knew they were references that were frowned upon—although intellectually tolerated. (Yes, I instinctively understood the distinction.) One thing I understood from my grandmother: our faith was for everyday use, not simply Sunday attendance at a beautiful church. I felt this made sense, and indeed it became nothing less than the foundation of my identity and my values. I sense that this profound belief also lay deep within my grandfather, even if we never talked about it."

He said he usually walked with his grandmother to St. John's, Lafayette Square, or sometimes they drove to St. Thomas' and, occasionally, churches of other denominations. When the president was with them, it was "more showy" with an open car and motorcycle escort.[29]

Eleanor explained, "My husband didn't go to church much then because he found it too painful to put the braces on. They were *terrible*! And also, he didn't like the fact that so many Secret Service men had to accompany him." Each year on the anniversary of his inauguration he had the clergy hold a special service in the White House. "I think it shows the confidence that the people had in Franklin that there was never a word of protest against his having religious services in the President's house."[30]

For the remainder of her life, Eleanor would continue to write and speak, actively promoting the United Nations around the world and providing concrete support for the civil rights movement in the United States, to the point of providing bail money for Martin Luther King Jr. when his nonviolent demonstrations led to arrests. Her enduring commitment to racial equality led to lasting friendships with a number of exemplary Christians, who are not always recognized as such: Dr. King, as he is widely known, was a Baptist clergyman with a doctorate in theology; Pauli Murray was a devout Episcopalian and church organist who eventually became a priest; Thurgood Marshall was a cradle Episcopalian who has a feast day in the church's liturgical calendar; and Howard Thurman was a Baptist clergyman and prolific author, who was a spiritual advisor to both King and Murray. Eleanor had joined the Fellowship Church in San Francisco, which he had founded. In 1974, he was named an honorary canon of the Cathedral of St. John the Divine.

She would also continue expressing her reverence for the Bible. In 1944, she had donated to an American Bible Society campaign to provide Bibles around the world, especially to war-torn areas. In 1952, she was present for the roll out of the Revised Standard Version, and she endorsed National Bible Week in her column.

EPILOGUE

APPRECIATING THE RELIGIOUS LIFE OF ELEANOR ROOSEVELT

While biographers and admirers rightly appreciate Eleanor for her independence, her determination, her assertiveness, or her strength, few would describe her life as a life of obedience. It was not a life of subservience to human authority figures, to be sure. Instead, it was the radical attentiveness of which the mystics speak. In fact, it follows "stability," discussed earlier, as the second of the Benedictine vows that so profoundly shaped English Christianity in general and Anglicanism in particular. Eleanor's obedient listening gave her a reputation among those who knew her for having an ability to listen very closely to people and to formulate some kind of active response. Her response to Pauli Murray's first letter is an example. Only two days after she responded, she lifted up many of Pauli's concerns in her widely read column. Her response might take the form of guidance, but just as often it could be advocacy. It could be about helping one person or about helping whole groups of people. The impetus for this radical obedience can be seen in Jesus's words to Simon Peter in John 21:1–19, in which he asks three times if Peter loves him. When Peter responds affirmatively each time, Jesus responds with an instruction: "Feed my lambs" the first time; "Tend my sheep" the second; and "Feed my sheep" the third time.

The image of feeding lambs, especially lost lambs, comes to mind when we consider Eleanor's work with the Wiltwyck School. Founded in 1936 by the Episcopal City Mission with Eleanor's bishop, William T. Manning, as president, the school was located across the river from Hyde Park near Holy Cross Monastery. Its purpose was to provide a residential school for troubled African American boys. In the language of the day, they were considered juvenile delinquents or potential delinquents.

Eleanor had been a supporter from the beginning, but in 1942 she took on a more substantive role. In some ways a victim of its own success, the school had grown to the point where the city mission could no longer sustain it financially. Eleanor joined with her close friend Judge Justine Wise Polier, daughter of the celebrated Rabbi Stephen Wise of the Free Synagogue, and her own daughter, Anna, to assume control of the school. Its new charter as an interracial, nonsectarian organization could have been—and probably was—written by Eleanor herself. The purpose of the organization was to provide "moral and spiritual enlightenment, character development, correction of behavior problems, education and training for good citizenship."[1]

The school continued for another forty years until treatment models changed in favor of nonresidential settings. During Eleanor's time, however, there was one thing the school could count on—an annual picnic at Hyde Park for more than one hundred boys and the teachers and social workers who served them. She fed the lambs from Wiltwyck just as she had fed the four hundred garment workers from the Women's Trade Union League, just as she had fed all the neighbors at Campobello, just as she would feed the annual gatherings of the Hudson Shore Labor School. It was the "hospitality solution" writ large.

Sometimes the hospitality was just for family and friends, but those numbers were large too. And her obedience to the instruction, practical and concrete, was also abstract and philosophical. Her forthright advocacy of minimum wage laws and the economic rights enshrined in the Universal Declaration represent a kind of metaphorical feeding—a right to food, to be sure, but a right to hope, a right to envision a greater well-being and to pursue it.

Her obedience extends to other commands as well. "Do this in remembrance of me" is the commandment Jesus offers at the Last Supper, which becomes the foundation of the Eucharist. In this, we have the clearest example of Eleanor herself being fed in a way that engendered the strength for which she became known.

William Turner Levy, an Episcopal priest and literature professor whom Eleanor befriended late in life, recalled worshipping with her at St. James', Hyde Park. "I could not but sense her complete separation from all earthly ties, caught up in a loving absorption" of the liturgy. He said T. S. Eliot was the only other person he had ever seen so fully enraptured in the Eucharist.[2]

Eleanor's enduring concern for human dignity is another way she obeyed the instruction to "Tend my sheep." Even as a child, she participated in activities to brighten the lives of children less fortunate than she was, ways that recognized that we do not live by bread alone. That sip of sweetness in the eucharistic wine, which Christ—God incarnate—describes as his blood, is the very lifeblood of the universe, the thing that makes the world go round, as it were.

Although she could never be described as "pleasure seeking," she knew pleasure's role in making life worth living. She herself took pleasure in long walks in the country, in conversations and reunions with friends, and in trips to the theater. One historian said Eleanor "loved serene moments of introspection at the fireside or during a walk in the woods. She felt close to the changing seasons, to the blooming of dogwood, daffodils, and tulips, and to the quiet mystery of woods, which she always longed for when she was away in the city."[3]

Despite a consistent pattern of applying the teachings of Christ, despite her close relationship to the Episcopal Church, two erroneous interpretations persist in the biographical literature. The first is the notion that she was not seriously "religious." The second is that she was anti-Catholic. Both stem from her own words and actions.

In 1951, the Roman Catholic archbishop of Los Angeles had criticized Eleanor for comments she made on Edward R. Murrow's CBS radio program, *This I Believe*. She told listeners she was not sure whether she believed in an afterlife and that there was no harm in people making their own judgments about it. She did not challenge or deny the creedal formulation about the resurrection of the dead. She simply stated, with characteristic humility, that she was not sure what it meant. Many Episcopalians might do the same, feeling that lack of clarity about a particular belief does not necessarily mean weak or nonexistent belief.

The archbishop, however, took her statement to mean that she was an agnostic generally and, therefore, unfit to "fashion a bill of human rights" because it would lead to an atheistic or agnostic world.[4]

Yet in a conversation with Wiliam Turner Levy, she expressed relief that the young priest did not feel the circumstances of her father's death would be a barrier to his being in heaven, assuring her that God's judgment is more generous than any human being's. She spoke of her love for her father and her hope of seeing him again in the afterlife.[5]

The charge of anti-Catholicism stems mainly from her "press war" with Cardinal Francis Spelman of New York. Eleanor opposed federal funding for parochial schools on the ground of separation of church and state, but Spelman said it was based on anti-Catholic prejudice. He may not have known that in 1928, Eleanor chose not to work in her husband's campaign for governor of New York but opted to work in the presidential campaign of Al Smith. She said the kind of anti-Catholic propaganda she encountered had "disgusted" her. "If I needed anything to show me what prejudice can do the intelligence of human beings, that campaign was the best lesson I have had."[6] In her 1946 contribution to *Christianity Takes a Stand*, she described anti-Catholicism as "complete non-sense."[7]

Eleanor would probably say "non-sense" to the suggestion that criticism of a particular position favored by a particular clergyman amounted to prejudice against the clergyman's entire religion. She took her own bishop, William Thomas Manning, to task for reversing the vestry election at St. James', Hyde Park. Despite his presidency of her cherished Wiltwyck School and his long relationship with her family, she was furious that he objected to her son Elliott's election to the vestry on the grounds that he had been divorced. In a testy letter on White House stationery, she said she would never again set foot in a church in his diocese. She did not make good on the threat, but she never buried the hatchet.[8]

She did, however, bury the hatchet with Cardinal Spelman. Her niece recalled the summer afternoon in 1949 after the controversy had died down and public opinion had pronounced Eleanor the victor. A long black limousine with tinted windows made its way up the dusty drive to Val-Kill Cottage. Eleanor asked Tommy (her assistant Malvina Thompson) if they had invited someone to tea. They had not and were, in fact, struggling to find time to schedule a meeting with Eleanor's editor. Then a uniformed chauffeur rang the doorbell. Cardinal Spelman, they were told, wished to pay a call.

Eleanor graciously invited him to join them for tea. According to her niece, they spent the next hour exchanging pleasantries, never once mentioning the controversy. In fact, neither one ever mentioned it again.[9]

Another criticism of Eleanor Roosevelt, less harsh, perhaps, is that she was not an original or systematic thinker. "Mrs. Roosevelt was not a profound thinker, nor was she very original in the philosophical positions she took. . . . Social Christianity and a fundamental belief in democracy were the bases of her philosophy," biographer Tamara Hareven said.

> One can search in vain for a balanced system of thought in Eleanor Roosevelt. Even her admirers had to admit intellectual shallowness and the absence of a great mind. Her detractors were harsher: "She spreads a squid-like ink of directionless feeling. All distinctions are blurred, all analysis failed," said James Burnham. In a column written after her death, William F. Buckley Jr. quoted this statement and concluded: "Some day in the future, a liberal scholar will write a definitive thesis exploring the cast of Mrs. Roosevelt's mind by a textual analysis of her thought, and then history will be able to distinguish between a great woman with a great heart, and a woman of perilous intellectual habits." Frances Perkins passed a similar verdict, although in

a more affectionate tone: "Mrs. Roosevelt's sole claim to greatness was as 'a woman with a great heart.'"[10]

A simpler response is possible. She was not an original or systematic thinker. She was an Episcopalian. Anyone who knows the Episcopal Church knows that it does not produce breakthrough systematic theologians or cutting-edge interpretations. The principal gift of the Episcopal Church, and Anglicanism generally, is the capacity for *synthesis*—the ability to gather many different streams of thought from scripture, tradition, philosophy, experience—and integrate them into something that makes common, practical sense. Eleanor Roosevelt possessed this gift, and she shared it with the world.

Eleanor's sense of humor is also consistent with the religious tradition that shaped her. It was, after all, General Seminary professor Clement Clarke Moore who gave the world a playful metaphor for an indiscriminately gracious, gift-giving God in "A Visit from St. Nicholas." John Roosevelt Boettiger said Eleanor's sense of humor was one of the few aspects of his grandmother's character that had been inadequately recognized by her biographers. "She comes across in too many accounts as knowing and wise but sober. No one who heard her wonderful narration of Prokofiev's 'Peter and the Wolf' would believe that. Nor anyone who sat around the table at a rambunctious family dinner at her home."[11]

Boettiger lived with his grandmother in Hyde Park for a few years and recalled entering her room after midnight one time to find her listening to Gregorian chant on the phonograph while finishing up the details of her day's work. During those years he noted he often drove her to St. James' Church. She was happy to attend by herself if she had no guests or family who wanted to come along, but quite often she had a variety of company sitting in the Roosevelt pew, ranging from the King and Queen of England to union leader Walter Reuther.

At that time, when the 1928 Prayer Book was still in use, there were quite a few "ups and downs"—kneeling for all prayers, standing for hymns and the reading of the Gospel, and sitting for other readings and for the sermon. Reuther, a lapsed Lutheran, relied on Eleanor for cues as to when to change posture. His daughter Elizabeth recalled that on the family's last visit, her father was at a loss because Eleanor had fallen asleep in the pew! When he woke her up, she chuckled and said, "Perhaps Franklin's prayer has finally been answered." The joke was that FDR used to pray that the ever-energetic Eleanor might occasionally get tired.[12] After the life she led, in fact, the life she gave to all humanity, surely no one would begrudge her a bit of rest.

Anna Eleanor Roosevelt died at the age of seventy-eight on November 7, 1962. Her funeral at St. James' was attended by President and Mrs. Kennedy, Vice President and Mrs. Johnson, former Presidents Eisenhower and Truman with Mrs. Truman and their daughter, New York Governor Nelson Rockefeller, and many other dignitaries.

She was buried next to her husband in the family cemetery on the Springwood estate, with their famous dog, Fala, close by. At the graveside service, the Rev. Dr. Gordon Kidd, rector of St. James', described her as a "seeker who found a truth that made us all free."[13]

After the funeral, memorial services were hosted by both the Cathedral of St. John the Divine and Washington Cathedral. Both services were attended by the whole family, according to son Elliott. "New York gave an opportunity for a lot of the UN diplomats and employees. Most members of the House and Senate, the cabinet, the Supreme Court, and government workers attended Washington," where Secretary of State Dean Rusk delivered the eulogy.

At St. John the Divine, Eleanor's devoted friend Adlai Stevenson told ten thousand mourners that Mrs. Roosevelt possessed a "luminous faith that testified always for sanity in an insane time and for hope in a time of obscure hope."[14] A week earlier in an address to the United Nations General Assembly, he had offered the remark that has lived in memory: "She would rather light candles than curse the darkness, and her glow has warmed the world."[15]

ENDNOTES

INTRODUCTION

1. Elliott Roosevelt and James Brough, *Mother R: Eleanor Roosevelt's Untold Story* (Putnam, 1977).
2. Eleanor Roosevelt, *The Autobiography of Eleanor Roosevelt* (Da Capo Press, Inc., 1992), xv.
3. R. Maas, "Narrative Theology," in *New Catholic Encyclopedia*, 2nd ed. (Thomson Gale and Catholic University of America, 2003), 151–54.
4. J. H. Randolph Ray, *My Little Church Around the Corner* (Simon and Schuster, 1957), 173.

CHAPTER ONE

1. Harold Ivan Smith, *Eleanor: A Spiritual Biography* (Westminster John Knox Press, 2017), 11.
2. Roosevelt and Brough, *Mother R*, 151–152.
3. Eleanor Roosevelt, "My Day, March 6, 1940," *The Eleanor Roosevelt Papers*, digital edition, https://www2.gwu.edu/~erpapers/myday/displaydoc.cfm?_y=1940&_f=md055520, accessed July 3, 2025.

4. Roosevelt, *The Autobiography of Eleanor Roosevelt*, 4.
5. Joseph Lash, *Eleanor and Franklin* (W. W. Norton & Company, 1971), 17.
6. Lash, *Eleanor and Franklin*, 27.
7. Lash, *Eleanor and Franklin*, 5.
8. James Elliott Lindsley, *This Planted Vine: A Narrative History of the Episcopal Diocese of New York* (Harper & Row Publishers, 1984), 197–98.
9. Roosevelt, *The Autobiography of Eleanor Roosevelt*, 12.
10. Roosevelt, *The Autobiography of Eleanor Roosevelt*, 13.
11. Roosevelt, *The Autobiography of Eleanor Roosevelt*, 13.
12. Richard G. Hewlett, "The Creation of the Diocese of Washington and Washington National Cathedral," *Anglican and Episcopal History* (September 2002): 350–79.
13. Henry Yates Satterlee, *Life Lessons from the Prayer Book* (James Pott & Co. Publishers, 1889), iii–iv.
14. Lash, *Eleanor and Franklin*, 391.
15. J. Newton Perkins, *History of the Parish of the Incarnation, New York City, 1852–1912* (Frank B. Howard Press, 1912), 257.
16. William M. Grosvenor, *Four Sermons* (Thomas Whitaker, n.d.), https://anglicanhistory.org/usa/wmgrosvenor/four_sermons.html, accessed January 5, 2025.
17. Grosvenor, *Four Sermons.*
18. Grosvenor, *Four Sermons.*
19. Eleanor Roosevelt, *The Moral Basis of Democracy* (Howell, Soskin & Co., 1940), 56.
20. Eleanor Roosevelt, *The Moral Basis of Democracy*, 57.
21. Grosvenor, *Four Sermons.*
22. Lash, *Eleanor and Franklin*, 17.
23. "Mary Livingston Ludlow Hall (1843–1919)," Eleanor Roosevelt Papers Project, https://erpapers.columbian.gwu.edu/mary-livingston-ludlow-hall-1843-1919, accessed January 14, 2025.

24. Smith, *Eleanor*, 4.
25. Roosevelt, *The Autobiography of Eleanor Roosevelt*, 105.
26. William M. Grosvenor, Puritan Remnant, December 17, 1911, https://anglicanhistory.org/usa/wmgrosvenor.

CHAPTER TWO

1. Lash, *Eleanor and Franklin*, 16.
2. Lash, *Eleanor and Franklin*, 3.
3. Eleanor Roosevelt, *You Learn by Living: Eleven Keys for a More Fulfilling Life* (Harper Perennial, 2011), 3.
4. Roosevelt, *The Autobiography of Eleanor Roosevelt*, 6–8.
5. David Michaelis, *Eleanor* (Simon & Schuster, 2020), 13.
6. Roosevelt, *You Learn by Living*, 3–4.
7. Lash, *Eleanor and Franklin*, 15.
8. Roosevelt, *You Learn by Living*, 4.
9. Lash, *Eleanor and Franklin*, 22.
10. Smith, *Eleanor*, 23.
11. Roosevelt, *The Autobiography of Eleanor Roosevelt*, 6–7.
12. Roosevelt, *The Autobiography of Eleanor Roosevelt*, 6–7.
13. Blanche Wiesen Cook, *Eleanor Roosevelt: Volume 1, The Early Years, 1884–1933* (Penguin Press, 1993), 38–56.
14. Cook, *Eleanor Roosevelt, Volume 1*, 59–62.
15. Lash, *Eleanor and Franklin*, 75.
16. Smith, *Eleanor*, 37.
17. Lash, *Eleanor and Franklin*, 73.
18. Lash, *Eleanor and Franklin*, 52.
19. Lash, *Eleanor and Franklin*, 79–81.
20. Matthew 18:1–5; Mark 9:33–37; Luke 9:46–48.
21. Smith, *Eleanor*, 43.
22. Lash, *Eleanor and Franklin*, 91–107.
23. Roosevelt, *You Learn by Living*, 28–29.
24. Smith, *Eleanor*, 46–47.

25. Smith, *Eleanor*, 44.
26. Smith, *Eleanor*, 45.
27. Smith, *Eleanor*, 53.
28. Roosevelt, *You Learn by Living*, 5.
29. Smith, *Eleanor*, 53
30. John Roosevelt Boettiger, "The Spirit of Eleanor Roosevelt," *Reckonings: A Journal of Justice, Hope and History*, January 16, 2019, https://www.reckonings.net/reckonings/2019/01/index.html.
31. "What Religion Means to Me," Eleanor Roosevelt Papers Project, https://erpapers.columbian.gwu.edu/what-religion-means-me, accessed January 15, 2025.
32. Roosevelt, *The Autobiography of Eleanor Roosevelt*, 2.
33. Roosevelt, *The Autobiography of Eleanor Roosevelt*, 30.
34. Eleanor Roosevelt, *Tomorrow Is Now* (Harper & Row, 1963), 119–120.
35. Roosevelt, *You Learn by Living*, 26.
36. Lash, *Eleanor and Franklin*, 10.
37. Roosevelt, *You Learn by Living*, xi.
38. Esther de Waal, *Seeking God: The Way of St. Benedict* (Liturgical Press, 2001), 60.

CHAPTER THREE

1. Roosevelt, *You Learn by Living*, 28.
2. Vida Scudder, *Father Huntington* (E. P. Dutton & Co., 1940), 162.
3. Kevin Phillips, *The Cousins' War: Religion, Politics, and the Triumph of Anglo-America* (Basic Books, 1999), xv.
4. John Winthrop, "A Model of Christian Charity," *A Library of American Literature: Early Colonial Literature, 1607–1675*, ed. Edmund Clarence Stedman and Ellen Mackay Hutchinson (Legare Street Press, 2022), 304–7.

5. Lash, *Eleanor and Franklin*, 33.
6. Lindsley, *This Planted Vine*, 211.
7. Dean Albertson, *The Reminiscences of Frances Perkins*, vol. 1, part 1 (Columbia University Oral History Project, 1951–55), 95.
8. James Edward Moore, *A History of the Church Association for the Advancement of the Interests of Labor* (General Theological Seminary, 1991). Also, Leonel Mitchell, "The Episcopal Church and the Christian Social Movement in the Nineteenth Century," *Historical Magazine of the Protestant Episcopal Church* 30, no. 3 (1961): 173–82.
9. George Hodges, *Henry Codman Potter, Seventh Bishop of New York* (Macmillan, 1915), 345–47.
10. "Bishop Potter Helps Dedicate Model Saloon," *The New York Times*, August 3, 1904.
11. Rabbi Joseph Silverman in *Memorial to Henry Codman Potter* (Cheltenham Press, 1909).
12. "Jews Have Been Liberal Towards Building of Churches, Cathedral Committee States," *Jewish Daily Bulletin*, December 31, 1924, https://www.jta.org/archive/jews-have-been-liberal-towards-building-of-churches-cathedral-committee-states.

CHAPTER FOUR

1. Bridgid O'Farrell, *She Was One of Us* (ILR Press, 2010), 7.
2. Rudy Abramson, *Spanning the Century: The Life of W. Averell Harriman, 1891–1986* (William Morrow and Company, 1992).
3. "The 1899 Expedition," PBS, www.pbs.org/harriman/1899/1899.html, accessed February 1, 2025.
4. "Harriman, Mary Williamson Averell," *Notable American Women, 1607–1950: A Biographical Dictionary*, vol. 2, ed. Edward T. James, Janet Wilson James, and Paul S. Boyer (Belknap Press, 1971).

5. Roosevelt, *The Autobiography of Eleanor Roosevelt*, 40.
6. Lash, *Eleanor and Franklin*,109.
7. O'Farrell, *She Was One of Us*, 8.
8. O'Farrell, *She Was One of Us*, 9.
9. O'Farrell, *She Was One of Us*, 8.
10. Lash, *Eleanor and Franklin*, 131.
11. Roosevelt, *You Learn by Living*, 41.
12. E. P. Newton, *Historical Notes of Saint James Parish, Hyde Park-on-Hudson* (A.V. Haight, 1913), 13.
13. Eleanor Roosevelt, "My Day, September 7, 1946," https://www2.gwu.edu/~erpapers/myday/displaydoc.cfm?_y=1946&_f=md000437.
14. Roosevelt, *You Learn by Living*, 33–34
15. Roosevelt, *The Autobiography of Eleanor Roosevelt*, 68.
16. The Cathedral of All Saints, History, https://www.cathedralofallsaints.org/history, accessed January 18, 2025.
17. Roosevelt, *The Autobiography of Eleanor Roosevelt*, 68.
18. "Eleanor Roosevelt: First Lady, League Leader, Pioneer, League of Women Voters," https://www.lwv.org/eleanor-roosevelt-first-lady-league-leader-pioneer, accessed February 2, 2025.
19. James Srodes, *On Dupont Circle: Franklin and Eleanor Roosevelt and the Progressives Who Shaped Our World* (Counterpoint, 2012), 7–9, 22.
20. O'Farrell, *She Was One of Us*, 12.
21. O'Farrell, *She Was One of Us*, 12.
22. Roosevelt, *You Learn by Living*, 35.
23. Roosevelt, *You Learn by Living*, 30.
24. Roosevelt, *The Autobiography of Eleanor Roosevelt*, 92.
25. Roosevelt, *The Autobiography of Eleanor Roosevelt*, 261.
26. Roosevelt, *The Autobiography of Eleanor Roosevelt*, 82.
27. O'Farrell, *She Was One of Us*, 13.
28. O'Farrell, *She Was One of Us*, 16–20.

29. O'Farrell, *She Was One of Us*, 20.
30. Kirstin Downey, *The Woman Behind the New Deal: The Life and Legacy of Frances Perkins* (Anchor Books, 2009), 69–71.
31. Roosevelt, *The Autobiography of Eleanor Roosevelt*, 148.
32. O'Farrell, *She Was One of Us*, 5.

CHAPTER FIVE

1. Lash, *Eleanor and Franklin*, 437.
2. Susan Quinn, *Eleanor and Hick: The Love Affair That Shaped a First Lady* (Penguin Press, 2016), 44–45.
3. Smith, *Eleanor*, 86–87.
4. Smith, *Eleanor*, 90.
5. Albertson, *The Reminiscences of Frances Perkins*.
6. Roosevelt, *You Learn by Living*, 2–3.
7. Lash, *Eleanor and Franklin*, 439.
8. Henry van Dyke, *Foot-Path to Peace* (Dodge Publishing Co., 1910), https://www.loc.gov/item/31030390/.
9. Lash, *Eleanor and Franklin*, 438.
10. Smith, *Eleanor*, 89–90.
11. Paul M. Sparrow, "Eleanor Roosevelt's Battle to End Lynching," National Archives, FDR Library, February 12, 2016, https://fdr.blogs.archives.gov/2016/02/12/eleanor-roosevelts-battle-to-end-lynching.
12. Blanche Wiesen Cook, "'Turn Toward Peace': ER and Foreign Affairs," *Without Precedent: The Life and Career of Eleanor Roosevelt*, ed. Joan Hoff Wilson and Marjorie Lightman (Indiana University Press, 1984), 112.
13. Elaine M. Anderson, "Eleanor and The Bok Peace Prize," *Historical Perspectives: Santa Clara University Undergraduate Journal of History, Series II* Vol. 9, Article 7 (2004): 1–14.
14. Cook, *Eleanor Roosevelt, Volume 1*, 344.

15. The Book of Common Prayer (The Church Pension Fund, 1928), 44.
16. The Book of Common Prayer (1928), 36.
17. The Book of Common Prayer (1928), 43, 44.
18. The Hymnal, as authorized and approved by the General Convention of the Protestant Episcopal Church in the United States of America in the year of our Lord 1916, (Church Pension Fund, 1916).
19. The Hymnal of the Protestant Episcopal Church in the United States of America 1940, (Church Pension Fund, 1943).
20. Smith, *Eleanor*, 1–2.
21. Patricia Bell-Scott, *The Firebrand and the First Lady: Portrait of a Friendship* (Alfred A. Knopf, 2016), xvii.
22. Bell-Scott, *The Firebrand and the First Lady*, 345.
23. Bell-Scott, *The Firebrand and the First Lady*, 27–30.
24. Ruth Schmidt, "My Name Is Pauli Murray" (Fuller Studio, n.d.), https://fullerstudio.fuller.edu/my-name-is-pauli-murray.
25. Pauli Murray Center, *Who Is Pauli Murray?*, https:// https://www.paulimurraycenter.com/, accessed July 11, 2025.
26. Bell-Scott, *The Firebrand and the First Lady*, 132–33.
27. Schmidt, "My Name Is Pauli Murray."
28. Bell-Scott, *The Firebrand and the First Lady*, 348.
29. Eleanor Roosevelt, "My Day, December 16, 1938," https://www2.gwu.edu/~erpapers/myday/displaydoc.cfm?_y=1938&_f=md055138.
30. Eleanor Roosevelt, "My Day, April 10, 1939," https://www2.gwu.edu/~erpapers/myday/displaydoc.cfm?_y=1939&_f=md055236.
31. Roosevelt, *The Autobiography of Eleanor Roosevelt*, 189–90.
32. Roosevelt, *The Autobiography of Eleanor Roosevelt*, 189–90.
33. Lash, *Eleanor and Franklin*, 812.
34. Lash, *Eleanor and Franklin*, 822.
35. Roosevelt, *The Autobiography of Eleanor Roosevelt*, 233.

36. Shannon McKenna Schmidt, *The First Lady of World War II: Eleanor Roosevelt's Journey to the Frontlines and Back* (Sourcebooks, 2023), xii.
37. Schmidt, *The First Lady of World War II*, xiii.
38. Schmidt, *The First Lady of World War II*, 187.
39. Eleanor Roosevelt, "My Day, February 2, 1946," https://www2.gwu.edu/~erpapers/myday/displaydoc.cfm?_y=1946&_f=md000252.

CHAPTER SIX

1. Mary Ann Glendon, *A World Made New: Eleanor Roosevelt and the Universal Declaration of Human Rights* (Random House, 2001), 25.
2. Luke 1:30 (KJV).
3. O Farrell, *She Was One of Us*, 44–45.
4. O Farrell, *She Was One of Us*, 31.
5. Schmidt, *The First Lady of World War II*, 271.
6. Author's interview with Betty Spain (Klein), circa 1995, Church of the Holy Apostles, New York City, NY.
7. Bill of Rights Institute, "Eleanor Roosevelt and the United Nations," https://billofrightsinstitute.org/essays/eleanor-roosevelt-and-the-united-nations, accessed January 2, 2025.
8. Glendon, *A World Made New*, 25.
9. Glendon, *A World Made New*, xvi.
10. United Nations, "Preamble," https://www.un.org/en/about-us/un-charter/preamble, accessed July 18, 2025.
11. Eleanor Roosevelt, "My Day, March 7, 1946," https://www2.gwu.edu/~erpapers/myday/displaydoc.cfm?_y=1946&_f=md000280.
12. O. Frederick Nolde, *Free and Equal* (World Council of Churches, 1968), 9.
13. Roosevelt, *The Autobiography of Eleanor Roosevelt*, 317.

14. Mary Ann Glendon, "God and Mrs. Roosevelt," *First Things*, May 2010, https://firstthings.com/god-and-mrs-roosevelt.
15. Eleanor Roosevelt, "My Day, December 25, 1951," https://www2.gwu.edu/~erpapers/myday/displaydoc.cfm?_y=1951&_f=md002100.
16. "Our History," Church Women United, https://www.churchwomenunited.net/history, accessed February 28, 2025.
17. Eleanor Roosevelt, "My Day, March 29, 1948," https://www2.gwu.edu/~erpapers/myday/displaydoc.cfm?_y=1948&_f=md000926.
18. Eleanor Roosevelt II, *With Love, Aunt Eleanor: Stories from My Life with the First Lady of the World* (Scrapbook Press, 2004), 78.
19. United Nations, "Universal Declaration of Human Rights," https://www.un.org/en/about-us/universal-declaration-of-human-rights, accessed July 18, 2025.
20. John S. Nurser, *For All Peoples and All Nations: The Ecumenical Church and Human Rights* (Georgetown University Press, 2005), 148–49.
21. "United States Proposals Regarding an International Bill of Rights," United Nations Economic and Social Council, January 28, 1947, https://docs.un.org/en/E/CN.4/4.
22. Michael S. Perry, *Labor Rights in the Jewish Tradition* (Jewish Labor Committee, 1993).
23. Doris Kearns Goodwin, *No Ordinary Time: Franklin and Eleanor Roosevelt: The Homefront in World War II* (Simon and Schuster, 2008), 102.
24. Blanche Wiesen Cook, *Eleanor Roosevelt: Volume 2, The Defining Years, 1933–1938* (Penguin Press, 2000), 316–17.
25. Glendon, *A World Made New*, 147.
26. United Nations, "Universal Declaration of Human Rights," https://www.un.org/en/about-us/universal-declaration-of-human-rights, accessed July 18, 2025.

27. Lynnaia Main, "History of The Episcopal Church and the United Nations," The Episcopal Church, https://www.episcopalchurch.org/ministries/global-partnerships/episcopal-church-united-nations/history, accessed March 1, 2025.
28. Eleanor Roosevelt, "The Minorities Question," *Christianity Takes a Stand*, ed. William Scarlett (Penguin Books, 1946), 72–76.
29. Curtis Roosevelt, *Upstairs at the Roosevelts': Growing Up with Franklin and Eleanor* (Potomac Books, 2017), 90–94.
30. William Turner Levy and Cynthia Eagle Russett, *The Extraordinary Mrs. R: A Friend Remembers Eleanor Roosevelt* (John Wiley & Sons, 1999), 26.

EPILOGUE

1. Wiltwyck School for Boys Records, 1942–1981, Rare Book and Manuscript Library, Columbia University, https://www.columbia.edu/cu/libraries/inside/projects/findingaids/scans/pdfs/WiltwyckSchool.pdf.
2. Levy and Russett, *The Extraordinary Mrs. R*, 240.
3. Tamara K. Hareven, *Eleanor Roosevelt: An American Conscience* (Quadrangle Books, 1968), xviii.
4. Michaelis, *Eleanor*, 526.
5. Geoffrey Ward, *Before the Trumpet: Young Franklin Roosevelt 1882–1905* (Harper and Row, 1985), 287.
6. Roosevelt, *The Autobiography of Eleanor Roosevelt*, 148.
7. Roosevelt, "The Minorities Question," 73.
8. William Thomas Manning Papers, box 25, folder 1, no. 10, The General Theological Seminary Manuscript Collection, n.d.
9. Roosevelt II, *With Love, Aunt Eleanor*, 100.
10. Hareven, *Eleanor Roosevelt*, xvii–xviii, 266.
11. Boettiger, "The Spirit of Eleanor Roosevelt."

12. Elizabeth Reuther Dickmeyer, *Reuther: A Daughter Strikes* (Spelman Publishers Division, 1989), 107–118.
13. The Reverend Gordon L. Kidd, quoted in "Eleanor Roosevelt Rites Held at Hyde Park," *The New York Times*, November 10, 1962, sec. A, p. 11.
14. Carleton W. Sterling, *Columbia Daily Spectator*, vol. CVII, no. 32, November 19, 1962.
15. "Eleanor Roosevelt Eulogized by Adlai," *Chicago Daily Tribune*, part 1, page 5, November 10, 1962.

BIBLIOGRAPHY

Abramson, Rudy. *Spanning the Century: The Life of W. Averell Harriman, 1891–1986*. William Morrow & Co., 1992.

Albertson, Dean. *The Reminiscences of Frances Perkins*. Columbia University Oral History Project, 1951–55.

Anderson, Elaine M. "Eleanor and The Bok Peace Prize." *Historical Perspectives: Santa Clara University Undergraduate Journal of History, Series II* Vol. 9, Article 7 (2004): 1–14.

Bell-Scott, Patricia. *The Firebrand and the First Lady: Portrait of a Friendship*. Alfred A. Knopf, 2016.

Bill of Rights Institute. "Eleanor Roosevelt and the United Nations." https://billofrightsinstitute.org/essays/eleanor-roosevelt-and-the-united-nations, accessed March 15, 2025.

Black, Ruby A. *Eleanor Roosevelt: A Biography*. Sloan and Pearce, 1940.

Boettiger, John Roosevelt. "The Spirit of Eleanor Roosevelt." *Reckonings: A Journal of Justice, Hope and History* (January 16, 2019). https://www.reckonings.net/reckonings/2019/01/index.html.

Cook, Blanche Wiesen. *Eleanor Roosevelt: Volume 1, The Early Years, 1884–1933*. Penguin Press, 1993.

Cook, Blanche Wiesen. *Eleanor Roosevelt: Volume 2, The Defining Years, 1933–1938*. Penguin Press, 2000.

Cook, Blanche Wiesen. *Eleanor Roosevelt, Volume 3: The War Years and After, 1939–1962*. Viking Press, 2016.

Cook, Blanche Wiesen. "'Turn Toward Peace': ER and Foreign Affairs." In *Without Precedent: The Life and Career of Eleanor Roosevelt*, edited by Joan Hoff Wilson and Marjorie Lightman. Indiana University Press, 1984.

De Waal, Esther. *Seeking God: The Way of St. Benedict*. Liturgical Press, 2001.

Dickmeyer, Elizabeth Reuther. *Reuther: A Daughter Strikes*. Spelman Publishers Division, 1989.

Downey, Kirstin. *The Woman Behind the New Deal: The Life and Legacy of Frances Perkins*. Anchor Books, 2009.

Eleanor Roosevelt Papers Project. George Washington University, Columbian College of Arts and Sciences, Washington, D.C.

Glendon, Mary Ann. "God and Mrs. Roosevelt." *First Things*, May 2010. https://firstthings.com/god-and-mrs-roosevelt/.

Glendon, Mary Ann. *A World Made New: Eleanor Roosevelt and the Universal Declaration of Human Rights*. Random House, 2001.

Goodwin, Doris Kearns. *No Ordinary Time: Franklin and Eleanor Roosevelt: The Homefront in World War II*. Simon and Schuster, 2008.

Grosvenor, William M. *Four Sermons*. Thomas Whitaker, n.d. https://anglicanhistory.org/usa/wmgrosvenor/four_sermons.html.

Hareven, Tamara K. *Eleanor Roosevelt: An American Conscience*. Quadrangle Books, 1968.

Hewlett. Richard G. "The Creation of the Diocese of Washington and Washington National Cathedral." *Anglican and Episcopal History* 71, no. 3 (September 2002): 350–79.

Hodges, George. *Henry Codman Potter, Seventh Bishop of New York*. Macmillan, 1915.

James, Edward T., Janet Wilson James, and Paul S. Boyer, eds. *Notable American Women, 1607–1950: A Biographical Dictionary.* Belknap Press, 1971.

"Jews Have Been Liberal Towards Building of Churches, Cathedral Committee States." *Jewish Daily Bulletin.* Jewish Telegraphic Agency. December 31, 1924. https://www.jta.org/archive/jews-have-been-liberal-towards-building-of-churches-cathedral-committee-states.

Kujawa-Holbrook, Sheryl A. *Freedom Is a Dream: A Documentary History of Women in the Episcopal Church.* Church Publishing, 2002.

Lash, Joseph. *Eleanor and Franklin.* W. W. Norton & Company, 1971.

Levy, William Turner, and Cynthia Eagle Russett. *The Extraordinary Mrs. R: A Friend Remembers Eleanor Roosevelt.* John Wiley & Sons, Inc., 1999.

Lindsley, James Elliott. *This Planted Vine: A Narrative History of the Episcopal Diocese of New York.* Harper & Row, Publishers, 1984.

Maas, R. "Narrative Theology." In *New Catholic Encyclopedia*. 2nd ed. Thomson Gale and Catholic University of America, 2003.

Michaelis, David. *Eleanor*. Simon & Schuster, 2020.

Mitchell, Leonel L. "The Episcopal Church and the Christian Social Movement in the Nineteenth Century." *Historical Magazine of the Protestant Episcopal Church* 30, no. 3 (1961): 173–82.

Moore, James Edward. *A History of the Church Association for the Advancement of the Interests of Labor*. General Theological Seminary, 1991.

Main, Lynnaia. "History of The Episcopal Church and the United Nations." The Episcopal Church. https://www.episcopalchurch.org/ministries/global-partnerships/episcopal-church-united-nations/history, accessed March 1, 2025.

Newton, E. P. *Historical Notes of Saint James Parish, Hyde Park-on-Hudson*. A. V. Haight, 1913.

Nolde, O. Frederick. *Free and Equal*. World Council of Churches, 1968.

Nurser, John S. *For All Peoples and All Nations: The Ecumenical Church and Human Rights*. Georgetown University Press, 2005.

O'Farrell, Bridgid. *She Was One of Us: Eleanor Roosevelt and the American Worker*. ILR Press, 2010.

Pauli Murray Center. *Who Is Pauli Murray?*, https://paulimurraycenter.com, accessed July 11, 2025.

Perkins, J. Newton. *History of the Parish of the Incarnation, New York City, 1852–1912*. Frank B. Howard Press, 1912.

Perry, Michael S. *Labor Rights in the Jewish Tradition*. Jewish Labor Committee, 1993.

Phillips, Kevin. *The Cousins' Wars: Religion, Politics, and the Triumph of Anglo-America*. Basic Books, 1999.

The Protestant Episcopal Church. The Book of Common Prayer and Administration of the Sacraments and Other Rites and Ceremonies of the Church: Together with the Psalter or Psalms of David According to the Use of the Episcopal Church. Eyre and Spottiswoode, 1892. http://justus.anglican.org/resources/bcp/1892/BCP_1892.htm.

The Protestant Episcopal Church. The Book of Common Prayer and Administration of the Sacraments and Other Rites and Ceremonies of the Church: Together with the Psalter or Psalms of David According to the Use of the Episcopal Church. Church Pension Fund, 1928. http://justus.anglican.org/resources/bcp/1928/BCP_1928.htm.

The Protestant Episcopal Church. *The Hymnal: as authorized and approved by the General Convention of the Protestant Episcopal Church in the United States of America in the year of our Lord 1916*. Church Pension Fund, 1916.

The Protestant Episcopal Church. *The Hymnal of the Protestant Episcopal Church in the United States of America 1940*. Church Pension Fund, 1943.

Quinn, Susan. *Eleanor and Hick: The Love Affair That Shaped a First Lady*. Penguin Press, 2016.

Ray, J. H. Randolph. *My Little Church Around the Corner*. Simon and Schuster, 1957.

Roosevelt, Curtis. *Upstairs at the Roosevelts': Growing Up with Franklin and Eleanor*. Potomac Books, 2017.

Roosevelt, Eleanor. *The Autobiography of Eleanor Roosevelt*. Da Capo Press, 1992. (Originally published by Harper & Brothers, 1961, and incorporating *This Is My Story*, *This I Remember*, and *On My Own*).

Roosevelt, Eleanor. "The Minorities Question." In *Christianity Takes a Stand*, edited by William Scarlett. Penguin Books, 1946.

Roosevelt, Eleanor. *The Moral Basis of Democracy*. Howell, Soskin & Co., 1940.

Roosevelt, Eleanor. "My Day." Eleanor Roosevelt Papers Project. https://erpapers.columbian.gwu.edu/my-day.

Roosevelt, Eleanor. *Tomorrow Is Now*. Harper & Row, 1963.

Roosevelt, Eleanor. "What Religion Means to Me." *Forum* 88 (December 1932): 322–24.

Roosevelt, Eleanor. *You Learn by Living: Eleven Keys for a More Fulfilling Life*. Harper Perennials, 2011.

Roosevelt, Eleanor, II. *With Love, Aunt Eleanor: Stories from My Life with the First Lady of the World*. Scrapbook Press, 2004.

Roosevelt, Elliott. *Eleanor Roosevelt, with Love: A Centenary Remembrance*. E. P. Dutton, 1984.

Roosevelt, Elliott, and James Brough. *Mother R: Eleanor Roosevelt's Untold Story*. Putnam, 1977.

Satterlee, Henry Yates. *Life Lessons from the Prayer Book: A Manual of Instruction for Bible Classes*. James Pott & Co. Publishers, 1889.

Scarlett, William, ed. *Christianity Takes a Stand*. Penguin Books, 1946.

Schmidt, Ruth. "My Name Is Pauli Murray." Fuller Studio, n.d. https://fullerstudio.fuller.edu.

Schmidt, Shannon McKenna. *The First Lady of World War II: Eleanor Roosevelt's Journey to the Frontlines and Back.* Sourcebooks, 2023.

Scudder, Vida. *Father Huntington*. E. P. Dutton & Co., 1940.

Silverman, Rabbi Joseph, *Memorial to Henry Codman Potter*. Cheltenham Press, 1909.

Smith, Harold Ivan. *Eleanor: A Spiritual Biography; The Faith of the 20th Century's Most Influential Woman*. Westminster John Knox Press, 2017.

Sparrow, Paul M. "Eleanor Roosevelt's Battle to End Lynching," National Archives, FDR Library, February 12, 2016. https://fdr.blogs.archives.gov/2016/02/12/eleanor-roosevelts-battle-to-end-lynching.

Srodes, James. *On Dupont Circle: Franklin and Eleanor Roosevelt and the Progressives Who Shaped Our World.* Counterpoint, 2012.

The New York Times. "Eleanor Roosevelt Rites Held at Hyde Park." November 10, 1962, sec. A, p. 11.

Thompsett, Fredrica Harris, and Sheryl A. Kujawa-Holbrook, eds. *Deeper Joy: Lay Women and Vocation in the 20th Century Episcopal Church.* Church Publishing, 2005.

"United States Proposals Regarding an International Bill of Rights." United Nations Economic and Social Council. January 28, 1947. https://docs.un.org/en/E/CN.4/4.

van Dyke, Henry. *Foot-Path to Peace*. Dodge Publishing Co., 1910. https://www.loc.gov/item/31030390/.

Ward, Geoffrey. *Before the Trumpet: Young Franklin Roosevelt 1882–1905*. Harper & Row Publishers, 1985.

William Thomas Manning Papers, box 25, folder 1, no. 10, The General Theological Seminary Manuscript Collection, n.d.

Wilson, Joan Hoff, and Marjorie Lightman, eds. *Without Precedent. The Life and Career of Eleanor Roosevelt.* Indiana University Press, 1984.

Wiltwyck School for Boys Records, 1942–1981. Rare Book and Manuscript Library, Columbia University. https://www.columbia

.edu/cu/libraries/inside/projects/findingaids/scans/pdfs/WiltwyckSchool.pdf.

Winthrop, John. "A Model of Christian Charity." In *A Library of American Literature: Early Colonial Literature, 1607-1675*, ed. Edmund Clarence Stedman and Ellen Mackay Hutchinson. Legare Street Press, 2022.

INDEX